47 Biggest Mistakes
Made by Property Investors and How to Avoid Them

By Helen Collier-Kogtevs

www.realwealthaustralia.com.au

Date of publication: 2007

Collier-Kogtevs, Helen
47 Biggest Mistakes Made by Property Investors and How to
Avoid Them

Includes index.
ISBN 9 78098038 9609.

I. Real estate investment – Australia. I. Real Wealth
Australia (Firm). II. Title. III. Title : Forty-seven
biggest mistakes made by property investors and how to
avoid them.

332.63240994

Published in Australia 2007
by Real Wealth Australia Pty Ltd
PO Box 333 Preston Victoria 3072
info@realwealthaustralia.com.au
Printed in Australia by Watson Ferguson & Company
Cover designed by Penguin Blue
Photo by Deb Cochrane

Acknowledgements

To John Logar, our business mentor and coach, for giving me the inspiration to create this book. Your "out of the box" thinking and guidance has been amazing and timely. I am truly grateful for your unending support and encouragement on my continuing journey of discovery. You have played an instrumental role in my life and words cannot express my true thanks and gratitude for the directional inspiration you have brought into my life.

To Ed's mum, Helga Kogtevs, you are one of the most amazing and generous people I have had the pleasure of having in my life. You have shown me love and tolerance and in so doing have made a huge difference to my life. Thank you for all your love and support.

To Marius Woulfe, the father figure I never had, I will be eternally grateful for your teachings, wisdom and support during my younger years when I needed it the most.

I would also like to acknowledge Tania Morrison; you are the most inspiring person I have ever met. You prove that everything is possible.

Dedication

To my loving husband Ed Kogtevs
You are my soul mate, my rock, my foundation.
Without you life would be meaningless.

Table of Contents

Introduction

If someone had said to me a few years ago that I would be sitting on a multi-million dollar property portfolio today, I would have laughed and thought they were absolutely crazy because at the time, in my mind, it was utterly impossible to imagine. With the level of bad debt I had and no savings in the bank, I figured I needed more than a miracle to get out of the mess I was in.

I spent my 20s in debt. I owed thousands of dollars on a car loan, credit cards, and several outstanding speeding and parking fines. I literally worked to pay off bad debt, simply because I didn't budget my expenditure and couldn't control my finances. To compound the situation, I would treat myself to a shopping spree almost every week with a mindset that I worked hard and deserved it, even though I couldn't afford it. That's how my credit cards spiraled out of control, which led to debt collectors knocking on my door. I would use my tax returns (what little I got) to try and clear some of the spiraling debt, which often made no real difference. As I was approaching my late 20s, I'd look at my situation in despair, feeling I had nothing to show for the years I'd worked except for a huge debt that I couldn't control.

To make matters worse (financially speaking), I met my husband-to-be, Ed, who was separated from his now ex-wife and going through a messy divorce. Are any divorces ever neat? Anyway, the divorce dragged on for years, as they most often do, while the assets were identified and distributed in accordance with the legal processes of the time. At the end of it all Ed ended up with the contributions in his superannuation fund (which he can't access until retirement) and his ex-wife got the house and a little cash. That wasn't the end of it though, as Ed was still also required to pay spouse and child support payments, which made a significant dent in his salary. I remember how devastated Ed felt that at the prime of his life with a limited number of working years left, he'd have to start over again and build a new financial future. Together we were almost financially crippled, battling to make ends meet.

The family financial support payments went on for years after settlement and it was hard going, but we stuck together and in the end we got through it. The experience actually made us stronger and even more determined to create a financial future for ourselves. I now have a newfound appreciation for people who go through divorce.

During the divorce Ed and I were pretty well financially restricted with what we could and couldn't do. Our only escape was our camping trips which we took whenever we could. It was on one of these trips, when we were sitting around a campfire enjoying a glass of red, that we began to create our financial future. It was obvious our combined superannuation funds wouldn't be enough to provide us with the lifestyle we wanted in retirement, which begged the question: what did we need to do about it?

We talked at length and wrote down all the possibilities we could think of to create wealth and also how we could clear our bad debt and still enjoy a reasonable lifestyle. We considered all investment asset classes but in the end chose the old faithful 'bricks and mortar' residential property. We realised we didn't know much about property investing except that it involved spending hundreds of thousands of dollars each time a property was purchased. This made us anxious and fearful of losing everything we had because of the risk of making a poor selection of an investment property, so we decided that before we started we needed to get a proper education into how to successfully invest in property.

We bought some books that tickled our property investing taste buds (refer to recommended reading list in part 6 of this book) and attended some free property seminars. The books and seminars really opened our eyes to what was possible. We then signed up for a two-year property education program which really put a spark under our backsides. We were so excited and couldn't wait to share our plans with family and friends. A friend still reminds us today of how she thought we were "bloody idiots" when we told her how much we were about to spend on our property education. For the record, she too has since spent a similar amount on her property education and now also enjoys the benefits of a multi-million dollar property portfolio. By the way, she no longer thinks we were "bloody idiots"!

Telling friends and family what we were doing was our first mistake. In their concern to protect us from something they didn't understand themselves, they initially canned everything we said and did about property investing. Thank God we didn't pay any attention to them. I even shared with some of my colleagues what we were doing in the hope they'd be inspired enough to want to invest in property themselves. Ironically, it didn't work and today they're still in the rat race, doing what they've always done and getting what they've always gotten. Many years on, those same people have started asking us how we did it.

The second mistake I made in property investing was when I purchased my first property. The mistake was that I fell in love with the property and not the investment. I do have to say it wasn't hard to do. When you come from having bad debt most of your life and living from pay cheque to pay cheque to all of a sudden owning an asset, it's hard not to get emotionally attached. I really wanted to live in that house and was bitterly disappointed when I realised we couldn't because it needed rental income to be able to sustain the mortgage and expenses. Property investing is all about the numbers and the numbers wouldn't have stacked up had we chosen to live in it. Thank God I'm emotionally over that property now. The only property I get emotionally attached to these days is the home I now live in.

It wasn't until my eighth property purchase that people started to sit up, look and listen. Funnily enough it was with the eighth property that I made another mistake – buying sight unseen. I listened to what the sales agent told me about the property and purchased it without validating the information first. I got lazy and took shortcuts with my research. The cost of this mistake was that a positive cash flow property turned into a negative cash flow property overnight. Wow, it hit the back pocket hard and added to us nearly 'hitting the financial brick wall' – another mistake!

The upside to nearly hitting the financial brick wall, so to speak, was that in our effort to gain more borrowing capacity we learnt an enormous amount about property finance and how the banks and mortgage insurers work. At one of the property seminars we attended, we met a mortgage broker who, over time, was generous enough to provide us with a thorough education in property finance. It was at about this time that I discovered that property isn't really about bricks and mortar; it's really about finance.

Nearly hitting the financial brick wall had a domino effect in that we got to really understand the negative impact of not having a balanced portfolio of positive cash flow and negatively geared properties. Our portfolio was very negatively geared and although we were comfortably managing the mortgage payments, the banks decided we were a potential risk to them – one they weren't prepared to take. We desperately wanted to continue to purchase more properties, but the banks were saying "no deal". We ramped up our education in the hope of learning how to balance our portfolio, which we then knew would free up more borrowing capacity. We eventually worked it out and now have a positive cash flow portfolio that still provides us with borrowing capacity.

We have continued to develop our knowledge by constantly educating ourselves, which has put us in good stead as it has enabled us to go on and teach others how we're achieving successful results.

You might ask yourself, how can you create a successful property portfolio without making any mistakes? The short answer is you can't. Even the most experienced investors still make mistakes. Making mistakes is normal and inevitable but it's the big ones that can be disastrous. Understanding potential mistakes and their impact before they occur will help you prepare an avoidance strategy that will either eliminate or minimise the impact should things go wrong.

My wonderful husband Ed and I have made our fair share of mistakes over the years. We make a point in this book of sharing our successes and failures, and in doing so show how real investors deal with the challenges and frustrations of property investing.

In this book I will share with you my dumbest mistakes and how easily they could have been avoided had I just known how to deal with them when they occurred. Property investing is not rocket science – anyone can do it. Ed and I are living proof of that. All you need is a little nouse and lots of determination and passion. Passion for me is the key ingredient, as it keeps you going when life throws up its inevitable obstacles. It's so easy to quit when things go wrong yet it's the passion that propels you to keep going.

I used to think having a mentor or coach to support my investing was a little 'wanky' and was only for those who were lost or in need of direction. As we have progressed we have learnt more and more about how much we really don't know. It became increasingly obvious that we needed a mentor to help us understand all of the subtle nuances of property investing.

Many of my own personal challenges have been lessened by the contribution my mentors have made. As they have done it all before, they're able to offer absolute pearls of wisdom and guidance along the way. Their support has enabled me to think bigger and broader so I can take on life more fully. I'm now focused and open-minded and am exploring all that is possible in my life.

One of the key points this book emphasises is that in order to be successful you need to set goals for yourself. Not setting goals is akin to being on a rudderless ship. How do you know where you're going if you have no idea what you're aiming for? Mistake number 40 (don't be a wannabe forever) describes how many investors fail to set themselves goals and in so doing fail to achieve real wealth.

I certainly don't want to amass wealth and then lose it due to a mistake that could have been avoided had I educated myself more completely. Life is not a dress rehearsal and I want to create the wealth that will provide me with the means to continue my journey of discovery. Learning from others and their experiences has enabled me to fast track my journey to where I am today.

The purpose of this book is to explain the biggest mistakes property investors make and, more importantly, how to avoid them. I have tried to be solution orientated to give you ideas that may help you apply my knowledge and learnings in your future property investing.

Part 1 - Planning

Mistake 1 – Failing to budget

I have had a lot of people approach me saying that they would love to be able to buy an investment property but either do not have or cannot save enough to use as a deposit for purchasing a property. Unfortunately one of the truisms of life is that people tend to spend to their level of income rather than to what they actually need. If they get an increase in their pay they either upgrade something that they already have or buy something new. They won't save it if it kills them and it's usually spent before they get it. If they were to take a step back and properly analyse their spending habits and then create a spending budget that truly reflects their needs rather than their income, they would find that they actually do have the capacity to save and, with enough disciplined saving, will quickly be able to accumulate enough disposable income for a deposit on an investment property. Most people, if they really try, will be able to save at least 10 per cent of their income.

Investing in property without a budget can significantly and adversely impact on your lifestyle so it's really important you know exactly what your true living expenses are and, after paying these, how much of your income is left to support your property investing endeavours. Do you ever feel like you just work to pay bills? Do you have a comfortable level of income but are unsure where all the money has gone by the end of the week? Are your credit cards generally at their limits? Do you own a nice car? Do you have a plasma television? What about a PDA or a Blackberry? Do you exceed your internet usage each month? Do you upgrade your mobile phone plan regularly? What about pay TV? Do you and/or the kids get all the latest gadgets? What about clothes – always the latest brands? What about your social life, do you use credit cards to pay for your nights out and maybe even your holidays? Do you then spend the next 12 months paying off the debt? Do you smoke or drink? What about gifts for friends and family, are they expensive? What about speeding and parking tickets, do you regularly collect them?

By completing a budget planner, you will understand your spending habits. You will then have a very clear picture of your personal financial situation before launching into buying an investment property. Spending money is what we all enjoy doing. The significant difference is that many cannot afford to shop as often as they do. Mounting credit card debt has become a significant and worrying problem in western societies and the impact of this level of bad debt will come home to roost eventually.

People with high incomes are more likely not to have a budget. This is because they have a regular cash income from their jobs and/or businesses. What they do not plan for is a rainy day. People on lesser incomes are forced to manage their money better as there is not as much to go around and they need to make sure they cover all their bills. However 'credit' can put these people in precarious situations. More affluent people tend to spend more often and sometimes it takes a hard knock, such as an illness or loss of income, for them to realise just how vulnerable their situation really is. Yes, you may have all the relevant income insurances, however I do not know of any medical insurance company that covers people for colds and flus. If you are self employed, two or three weeks off with the flu can burn a sizable hole in your hip pocket.

One of my favourite books is *The Millionaire Next Door* by Danko and Stanley. Their study of the wealthy is eye opening. What I found most fascinating was the results of their research. They interviewed many supposedly wealthy people, yet most interestingly they defined wealth as being able to financially survive indefinitely should they stop working and/or running their own business. Can you imagine what life would be like if you stopped working today? Things would be okay for a short while, however most people (regardless of position or income) would only survive about one month. How scary is that? Our need to consume costs us dearly.

Solution
I am not advocating that you do not enjoy what life has to offer. Instead, I would prefer you budgeted so that you understand your level of disposable income and do not have to worry about the associated debt and can enjoy life without having to work longer to pay for it.

I am all about making the most of this magnificent life as we only get one shot at it. For that reason, I have added a budget planner to help you take a look at your finances. Refer to part 6 of this book. I have a friend who did this. She couldn't understand where all her money was going each week, yet by completing the budget planner it allowed her to isolate the leakages and correct the problem. Most of her money was being spent on expenses that could have been avoided. By taking a few simple steps her cash flow increased significantly, thus allowing her to go on and purchase an investment property.
Here are my tips on how you can increase your cash flow:

- Stick a 'no junk mail' sign on your letter box. This will stop you from being tempted when the sales are on.
- If you have a lead foot and like to speed, take your foot off the accelerator or use public transport. I understand that this can be a problem for some people (like me) who have a V6 and enjoy giving it a 'bit of stick' every now and again.
- Shop for clothes at factory outlets.
- Save a small amount each week for your annual holiday rather than use credit.
- Do you really need pay TV?
- Purchase birthday and Christmas gifts throughout the year instead of at the time you need them. This way you can purchase the gifts when sales are on, saving you dollars.
- Cancel your newspaper/magazine subscriptions for a while.
- Reduce the limit on your credit cards, the less you have the less you will spend.

Completing a budget is an excellent way to understand where your money goes. The budget planner provided will definitely go a long way to highlighting any cash flow leakages you may have. Having a budget and understanding your level of disposable income will assist you in your wealth creation.

See part 6 of this book for a budget planner.

Mistake 2 – Not leaving enough to live on

It saddens me when I hear people share their bad experiences about property investing. The bad experience is usually the result of not considering lifestyle as part of the investing equation.

A typical story goes something like this. An investor purchases a property that earns him $250 per week in rent, however the mortgage is $400 per week and the expenses another $50 per week. So to keep the investment property he needs to find $200 a week out of his pocket. After a while he may have a couple of maintenance issues to attend to while he continues to pay mortgage repayments, property management fees, rates and insurances. He continues to pay out for the property, but he reads in the papers that the market is flat or going backwards and he gets frustrated that his property is not creating wealth for him. In fact, it is costing him money to keep it. So what does he do? He puts an end to the nightmare, the headache, the very thing that deprives him of the extra dollars each week to spend on friends and family and he puts the property on the market. Does this sound familiar?

I know of investors who have gotten to this point and then sold, only to lose money on the deal because they had to pay the agent's selling fee and other selling expenses. Did they sell at a profit or did they sell at a loss? Generally they make a loss or just break even.

If this has been your experience, do you think you would encourage others to do the same thing? Definitely not! The next time property investing came up in conversation, what do you think your reaction would have been? You would become the person at social gatherings who complains and criticises anyone who gets into property investing. You become the person that successful investors avoid like the plague.

Solution

Consider your lifestyle! How much money per week do you want your wealth creation strategy to cost you? If you want to enjoy your lifestyle then you need to give careful consideration to what you are doing.

For example, a new investor who was just getting into the market had worked out that he wanted to spend no more than $50 per week out of his pocket. He was getting close to his twilight years and didn't want to be heavily negatively geared. With some mentoring from me, the result was that he purchased three properties:

1. a capital growth property that cost him $100 per week after tax;
2. a capital growth property that provided a positive cash flow of $10 per week after tax;
3. a cash flow property that provided a positive cash flow of $50 per week after tax.

Overall, this investor was able to purchase a property portfolio worth $1.2 million which only cost him $40 a week to sustain. How many times could he do that? The property portfolio has since grown in capital value by around 10 to 12 per cent per annum. For nearly $1.2 million in property assets, this investor now earns more than $120,000 per year and it only costs him $2080 per year. Not bad at all, and if you can do it correctly upfront and consider your lifestyle then growing real wealth is as easy as ABC!

Here's my tip: if you are a new investor with no investment properties, consider how much you want to spend per week out of your pay packet on your wealth creation strategy and look for investment properties that will provide you with the overall results without costing you more than you want.

If you are already an investor with two or more properties, your considerations will be different. This is because your properties may already be costing you each week and you may need to consider your lifestyle even further before you take on another investment. Therefore you need to do an analysis of your position and have a look at what revenue or cash flow you have to play with. This result will give you an idea of what direction you need to take in order to move forward.

For example, if your portfolio is costing you $200 overall per week and your finances are a little tight, you may need to consider adding some cash flow opportunities to balance your portfolio. Let's say you purchase a positive cash flow property earning you $50 per week after tax. The extra $50 per week cash flow could be put towards the cost of maintaining your portfolio. Therefore your $200 per week out-of-pocket expenses now becomes $150 per week out-of-pocket. The additional cash you earn from this investment could alleviate the pressure on your lifestyle. Whether you have one or many properties, the principle is still the same. It's all about balance and considering your lifestyle as part of the equation.

Mistake 3 – There's a reason why they're called experts

It's amazing to see so many investors purchase property without consulting their accountants or finance brokers until the deal is done. To have a panel of experts to refer to can be the difference between buying a great investment or a lemon. How do you know what the impact of your investment purchase will be on your finances if you do not consult with experts? What is the impact of that property purchase on your taxable income? How much money can you actually borrow? How much of your income will that new investment property require each week?

This is one mistake I have not made personally, however I see investors make it all the time. The benefit of our mentors has been that they have helped us not to make this mistake. They have even provided us with a great opportunity to use the same experts they use. We have found that better experts increased our level of knowledge and allowed us to leverage our opportunities even further.

One of the most common experts people fail to seek advice from are finance brokers or bank managers. I see this happen regularly. People that have gone and purchased an investment property, handed over a sizeable deposit and then discovered they cannot obtain the finance to complete the transaction. If you have made this mistake or know of someone who has, you would know that a conversation with a finance broker or bank manager before you sign the contract and hand over your deposit would save you many sleepless nights filled with worry and stress.

Solution
I can't stress enough the importance of having experts as part of your team. One of the most important questions to ask your panel of experts is whether they are investors themselves. How can they possibly know all the nuances of property investing if they do not practise it themselves?

Look at property investing as a business and the experts as your employees. The benefit is that you pay them only when you use them. Therefore you do not need to concern yourself with payroll taxes and staff amenities.

If you are very worried about their fees then you should not be a property investor. If the advice saves you thousands of dollars then don't concern yourself over a few hundred dollars.

If the expert is not working for you, then sack him/her and find one who will work with you and give you great advice. Do you think Donald Trump made his billions by knowing everything himself? Absolutely not! He relies on the expert knowledge of solicitors, accountants and financiers to grow his wealth. You too can do the same. Before you purchase an investment property, speak with your accountant and ask him/her what the impact of the purchase will be. Ask whether buying it in your name, a trust or company is better for you. Let them know what your long term intentions are with the property so they can advise you accordingly.

For example, young adults study and learn the theory of driving a car before going for their Learners Permit. In theory they may achieve 100 per cent accuracy on their test, however they don't know anything about driving a car until they sit in the driver's seat and practise driving. Practical experience is what makes them better drivers. The same principle can be applied to your panel of experts. They must be able to guide you from their own experience within the boundaries of the law.

Here's my tip: seek expert advice before you purchase your investment property and not after.

Mistake 4 – Waiting for the market to change

I hear this all the time, people waiting for the market to change before they start investing. I don't understand it. What are they waiting for exactly? What does 'waiting for the market to change' mean? If they are waiting for interest rates to change and they are on the way up as the market is buoyant, at what point (or should I say what year) are they thinking interest rates will come down?

The other comment I hear is people wanting to take 'baby steps' into getting into the market. Again, what does that mean exactly? When I hear of 'baby steps' I think of the pitter patter of tiny little feet. How does one take 'baby steps' into investing? You either take steps towards investing or you don't. The comment of 'baby steps' generally stems from one's uncertainty, which in my experience often leads to the same outcome – no action.

Waiting for the market to change or taking baby steps may lead to missed opportunities. For example, when Ed and I started investing some years ago, the market was booming. We purchased several properties at market value in areas we'd researched. We struggled to obtain discounts on properties as the market was hot. Our research showed we would achieve equity through capital growth, hence we did not worry too much about negotiating a huge discount as the majority of properties in the area that we were looking at were selling at the asking price. Had we not purchased those properties when we did, we would not have been able to get the capital growth, have them revalued and draw down on the available equity to go on and purchase more properties.

If we had waited for the market to change, we would have missed out on hundreds of thousands of dollars in capital growth and therefore shortchanged ourselves in growing our wealth.

Solution

To overcome this mistake, obtain an education in property investing as this may assist you in overcoming your fears about getting into the market. The best time to invest is right now. At the end of the day if you do your homework and end up having to pay full asking price for a property, don't worry too much. If selected correctly property is generally very forgiving. Just make sure your research tells you that it will have good capital growth over the next seven to ten years. I understand there may be some people cringing right now and that is okay with me.

When you are a new investor or have a couple of properties under your belt, sometimes it is best to get established or keep momentum than to fuss over trying to get the best discount every time. I would rather you purchase a property (at market value) growing at 10 per cent over the coming years than to pour your savings into a bank account earning you 4 per cent.

Let's assume a man purchases a $300,000 property using a cash deposit of $60,000. If the property grows at 10 per cent in the first year it would earn him $30,000 in capital growth that year. If the same investor put his $60,000 into a savings account earning 4 per cent per annum, the return would only be $2400 in the first year. In this example, property has given this man a ROI (return on investment) of 50 per cent as opposed to 4 per cent in a savings account.

Purchase price:	$300,000
Deposit:	$60,000
Capital growth:	10%
Wealth created:	**$30,000**

Cash investment:	$60,000
Interest per annum:	4%
Wealth created:	**$2,400**

By investing his cash with a bank and waiting for the market to change, he would have shortchanged himself by $27,600! Getting into the market now and not waiting for it to change would result in him growing his wealth by $30,000 per year compounding even while he sleeps! Imagine the figures if he went on to purchase two or three properties.

Here's my tip: make sure you have considered the following:
• do the research on your selected area(s)
• have an understanding of your financial position
• ensure the numbers stack up for you
• make sure it suits your lifestyle

Then get going.

Mistake 5 – Not having an exit strategy

An exit strategy is the back-up plan for when things go horribly wrong and you need to get out of it without huge financial and emotional loss. So many investors don't even know what an exit strategy is, let alone what to do if things go wrong.

Here are just some of the things investors do not consider:
What happens if you can't find a tenant?
What happens if the property burns down?
What happens if you lose your job and can't pay the mortgage?
What if interest rates go up?
What if your personal circumstances change?
What happens if your tenant doesn't pay the rent?

If you haven't devised an exit strategy for these types of situations, then you're not properly managing your investment. If you don't know how you are going to handle each and every disaster that could come along then you'll go round the twist worrying about whatever it is that you don't have an exit strategy for. Having an exit strategy will give you peace of mind and allow you to sleep peacefully at night.

When investing in property you are dealing with big dollars and it's not worth jeopardising your financial situation, lifestyle or relationships by incessantly worrying about situations that you have not planned an exit strategy for.

Many people contact me wanting to participate in our property mentoring programs yet their spouses or partners are afraid to borrow money. In fact they can't stand the thought of getting into more debt than they already have. The reason for this is that they haven't been educated into understanding the difference between good debt and bad debt. Once properly understood, people's fear of good debt quickly disappears and they begin to welcome good debt with open arms. Until this fear is overcome it just isn't possible to successfully build a property investment portfolio.

Nine times out of ten it is people's lack of understanding, education and exit planning that creates fear or brings them unstuck. Once people have been educated and understand all the nuances that lead to successful property investing, they gain the confidence to be able to appreciate just how low risk property investing can be.

Solution

I have known people who have jumped into the property market because that's what their friends are doing or to 'keep up with the Jones's'. They just buy something without fully understanding the consequences. The exit strategy is what gives you peace of mind today and tomorrow. Here are some suggestions for your exit strategy.

Insurances – this includes building, contents, landlords: if your investment property is worth hundreds of thousands of dollars and has an uncertain tenant, you would be wise to invest the few hundred dollars per year on insurances to cover the risk(s).

As part of your mortgage, your financier requires you to have building insurance, however building insurance does not cover you for any of the contents such as carpets, window furnishings, light fittings etc. Therefore you will need to obtain contents insurance as well. Your insurance company will advise you on how much contents cover you will require.

Most comprehensive landlords insurance policies will cover a number of what-ifs, including: the cost of any damage to the property caused by the tenant; the property being destroyed; tenant squatting and not paying their rent; tenant leaving without paying rent; loss of rent while damage is repaired; and legal liability. So should the tenant or the tenant's visitors misbehave or be injured in any way, at least you know your insurance policy will cover it. You will need to consult with an expert insurance agent to make sure you have the correct insurance coverage for your property.

Should you purchase an investment property as part of a complex, building insurance is generally covered under the body corporate insurance policy. But make sure the policy is adequate for your peace of mind and includes areas such as your car park and/or storage areas on your part of the title.

Here's my tip: you will need to clearly read the terms and conditions on your policy as insurance companies do vary greatly in what they will cover. And remember, if you pay peanuts, you are bound to get monkeys so make sure your policy has all the necessary inclusions.

Fixing interest rates – a method for guarding against interest rate rises is to fix your interest rates for three, five or ten years. The fixed interest rate is generally slightly higher than the variable rate but if interest rate peace of mind is what you want then this might be for you. If you are nervous about interest rate fluctuations, then fix all or part of your loan to ensure consistency in your costs. In this way you will know that the major portion of your property's expenses will be fixed for that period of time. Be careful however not to fix interest rates just before they are about to come down. About three years ago fixed interest rates were at an all time low at 5.99 per cent, which was lower than the 6.3 per cent variable rate. We were able to fix our mortgages at 5.99 per cent for five years, which has been quite good for us now that interest rates are around 7.3 per cent.

Lack of cash flow – people's circumstances change all the time and a way to minimise change from impacting on your cash flow, and hence your ability to pay out-of-pocket mortgage payments and expenses, is to plan ahead. If you are employed on a PAYE basis and own investment properties, you can discuss with your accountant how you can obtain your projected annual tax refund at each pay period in the form of reduced tax taken from your pay packet. This means you can increase your cash flow each week instead of giving it to the Australian Tax Office (ATO) and waiting until the end of the financial year to get it back.

This process can be initiated by lodging an application form with the ATO which, if approved, allows your employer to reduce the amount of PAYE tax that is taken from your salary/wages each pay period. It's sort of like prepaying your annual tax refund on a pay-period by pay-period basis. Many investors are not aware of this facility so seek your accountant's advice if you wish to pursue it. As part of your exit strategy, try saving the money for those rainy days when your investment property may require maintenance or is untenanted for a couple of weeks while you look for a new one.

I keep a bucket of money in an account just for such occasions. If, for some reason, I can't afford the mortgage for that month due to it being untenanted (it has never happened but just in case), that money is used which gives me peace of mind knowing that should anything go wrong, I will not run the risk of losing the investment property.

Here's my tip: write down every fear you may have about investing in property and try to come up with an exit strategy for each situation that could arise. You may need to seek expert advice as a sensibility check on some of your strategies. If you cannot overcome a fear by developing a workable exit strategy, even with the advice of experts, it may be best not to proceed with the purchase. You need to feel comfortable at all times with every aspect of the purchase.

Mistake 6 – Not doing your homework

Due diligence is the research done prior to making the purchase. It helps the investor work out whether the property is a good buy or a 'goodbye'. Many investors talk to the selling agent, ask a few questions and then make their decision and if they can obtain finance for the property, the transaction goes ahead. There are so many horror stories from investors who did not do their due diligence on the property before they bought it.

Here are some questions investors do not consider:
Where and how far away are the schools, shopping centres, medical practitioners/facilities and transport?
What is council's future plans for the area?
What kinds of developments are being planned for the area?
Who lives in the street?
What has been the capital growth of the area over the past twelve months, five and ten years?
What is the predicted growth for the future?

Has the property been tenanted before and for how long?
Is that type of property sought after by tenants?
What is the vacancy rate of the area?

For example, one horror story I came across was of an investor who purchased a property not knowing what the neighbours were planning. Three months after his purchase, the neighbours sold up to a developer who started building a five-storey apartment block next door. Had the investor done some due diligence prior to purchasing the property, there would have been no surprises and he could have chosen whether to proceed with the transaction or not.

Another horror story that comes to mind is that of an investor who purchased his/her first investment property, a block of four units on the advice of someone else only to find out later that the council rates were $1000 more than expected, and that the whole block needed a renovation that ended up costing $50,000 more than was originally quoted. In addition to this, two of the units were tenanted by drunks and local property managers refused to manage the property.

Another example of poor due diligence and its impact is a new investor who used a buyer's advocate to purchase an investment property because he was time poor. He paid nearly $8000 to the advocate for finding him the deal, which was an old block of units in the country that was 30 years old and had never been renovated.

The investor came seeking my opinion after the deal was done. My first question was had he seen the property and what condition was it in? Other than a few photos, he could not give me any information, as he had not seen it. I suggested it would be good for him (being a new property investor) to go and have a look at it. The response I received was very negative. He questioned why he should spend money on an airline ticket to see the property. When I also suggested he purchase a property analysis report to find out how that place would perform long term in terms of projected capital growth, he once again showed concern for spending money on such a report.

He had spent hundreds of thousands of dollars purchasing an investment property plus a fee to someone for finding him the property, a property that turned out to be something less than it was cracked up to be, and all because he couldn't find the time to undertake his own due diligence on the property.

Solution
You can start by driving around the area and seeing what is there. Try and put yourself in the shoes of a potential tenant and ask the questions, does the area have transport, schools and shops close by?

There are many websites where you can obtain free data about the demographics of the area that you are investigating. These websites will give you all sorts of valuable information from the population to how many people rent in that area. As these websites are free, there are no excuses for not checking them out.

Here are my tips:
Tip number one: do your own due diligence on each and every property before you buy it. It will help you validate the information you will get from sales agents and other people who have a vested interest in the sale. With the right education,

undertaking due diligence is not as difficult as you might think, in fact it's quite easy. Just remember shortcuts will cost you in the end, so do it properly and thoroughly.

Tip number two: when looking for the right area to buy in, look for an area where the rental population is greater than 30 per cent, as it will help ensure there are enough people in the area wanting to rent properties.

Tip number three: to find out what planned infrastructure is going on in the area have a look at the local council website, it is usually full of great information. Don't be afraid to ring the council and speak to the town planner or business development manager. They will inform you of the future plans the council has for the area. You will be amazed at how helpful they are to investors. Don't forget to ask if your neighbours are planning to sell to a developer who has plans to build a five-storey building next door!

Tip number four: information on capital growth in particular areas of interest can be gained from a number of good quality websites, but you will need to be careful that the owner of the website is getting information from a reputable source. The type of information you will be able to obtain from these sites will give you a guide as to the sort of capital growth that has occurred over the past 12 months plus an indication on how it will track in the future. Property investment magazines also provide valuable information on growth rates etc. and there are many great companies that specialise in property analysis that also provide capital growth projection reports for a small fee. Capital growth is important because it is what creates serious wealth for property investors. Cash flow properties put money in your pocket but generally do not have high capital growth rates. This is with the exception of mining towns, but these need to be treated differently as they are one-industry towns and the capital growth is subject to the vagaries of the performance of that particular industry.

Tip number five: how do you know if your property has been tenanted before – ASK! The sales agent should have a history of the property or at least know who the property manager was. Contact that property manager and ask about the property. Find out whether they liked managing the property (this will give you an idea of how much work there is for the property manager). As a rule, property managers do not like properties that require constant maintenance as it takes up a lot of their time.

You can also ask the property manager what the vacancy rate is in the area. You want to know if the property will take days or weeks to rent out. As an investor, you do not want to have your property untenanted for months and then have to lower your rent to get someone into the property quickly. A tenant paying for the mortgage is better than you paying for it so don't be afraid to lower the rent to get a tenant in. Find out from the property manager what features tenants in the area are asking for, this will help with sourcing a property that will rent very well. Also remember that booms don't last forever so if there is a rental glut, you want your property to be the most sought after in any market. Having the features tenants are looking for will help ensure your property remains constantly tenanted.

Refer to part 6 of this book for more information on due diligence and the key areas to consider.

Mistake 7 – Not looking at demographics

Investors underestimate the significance and importance of demographics when it comes to buying an investment property. Demographics include such things as the age of the population in an area, income levels, occupation, number of people in households and the size and structure of households, etc. Why is this information important? Well it indicates to you what type of investment property you need to buy to satisfy the population living in the area.

For example, we purchased an inner-city apartment off the plan. When we did some research into the area we found the majority of new apartments being built had two bedrooms and not many one-bedroom apartments. However when we looked at the demographics, we could see the majority of people renting in the area were single and living alone and projections were that the number of single people in the area was going to increase in the future. We had originally planned on buying a two-bedroom apartment but quickly changed our mind and ended up buying a one-bedroom apartment.

The result was that when we settled and took possession of the apartment, we had a tenant move in within 10 days and the apartment has been solidly rented ever since. On the other hand, we knew of investors who had purchased a two-bedroom apartment in the same complex who waited for months before they were able to secure a tenant.

Over the years I have had a number of investors say to me that they would like to purchase a property in an area that they had recently been holidaying in because it was a lovely place to visit.

The holiday area was abuzz with people basking in the sunshine and lapping up the warmer weather. The local restaurants and shopping precincts were filled with people enjoying the easy-going lifestyle.

I am always happy to review an opportunity with an investor. However in the majority of these cases, closer inspection of the demographics showed that many of the people living in the area were transient, meaning they were only staying for a short time and the industry was based around a single industry, usually tourism, which was seasonal in demand. The demographics also indicated that there were generally higher than normal populations of retirees in these areas when compared to the surrounding areas and that most of the people living in these areas were owner-occupiers. Therefore from our demographic research we were able to deduce that the rental market fluctuated significantly due to seasonal demand, that there were a number of vacancies because the market was oversupplied and that rents fluctuated due to seasonal demand for the units.

Solution
Demographics will really give you an insight into the characteristics of an area and what is projected to happen in that area in terms of population and the way people live. As an investor the aim is to purchase a property people like living in and will want to rent for a long time. Remember, short-term rentals generally result in more wear and tear on the property (i.e. higher maintenance costs) and will also have higher letting costs as the property manager will have to look frequently for new tenants.

Here's my tip: target the demographics in the area you are buying in and only purchase an investment property that suits the needs of the tenant population in the area. If one-bedroom apartments are more sought after by tenants then buy a one-bedroom apartment. This method helps keep your property rented continuously. Should your tenant leave, at least you will have peace of mind knowing that it will be relatively easy to find another one without having to incur a long vacancy period.

Another example of the prudent use of demographics when buying a property was when we purchased a three-bedroom house in a suburb where the majority of residents were professional couples or young families. It was important to us to come up with a list of inclusions to satisfy this type of prospective tenant. This included things like a dishwasher, a 900mm cook top, a fully fenced backyard, air-conditioning and a double lock-up garage for storage etc.

By understanding the demographics, it became obvious which type of tenant we were targeting and what the property needed to have in order to consistently attract good tenants. Make sure you consider this when making your investment purchases.

As for falling in love with the holiday destinations you visit, try not to purchase anything until you have returned home, long after you have returned home. Hey, I have done it too. As I love the hot weather, every time I visit the South Pacific I come back wanting to purchase a property there. It's easy to get caught up in the atmosphere of the holiday destination but it's important to review the area thoroughly as well as consult with your experts. This will help with keeping a level head and focusing on the facts rather than the emotion of the holiday.

Mistake 8 – A balancing act

You may well have heard from many a property advisor that if you invest in property, it must be in properties that are growth properties (i.e. properties that won't be able to support themselves fully and will therefore take money out of your pocket each week – negative cash flow). While we agree in principal to this theory, if you apply it continuously you will almost definitely hit the financial brick wall which is when banks won't lend you any more money because they will see you as a high-risk lender.

There is generally a lack of understanding from most property advisors that we know of the principles and importance of positive cash flow in the development of a balanced property portfolio. By a balanced property portfolio I mean a balance between positive cash flow properties and negative cash flow properties.

We personally nearly hit the financial brick wall at five capital growth, negative cash flow properties. The banks were getting nervous about lending us any more money until we discovered the impact that balancing our portfolio with positive cash flow properties had on our capacity to borrow more. We then purchased a whole string of positive cash flow properties that freed up our borrowing capacity and allowed us to purchase more growth properties.

I recently went along to a Robert Kiyosaki event where he talked about the importance of cash flow. My understanding of his message was that he could not understand why people would invest and have money taken out of their pocket. He went on to explain how his investments added money into his pocket, which he then used to fund his lifestyle.

Think of it this way; if you were running a business at a loss, how long would you survive before you were declared bankrupt? Yet if you believe some property advisors, it seems to be acceptable to them to buy properties that constantly take money out of an investor's pocket each week. Is it any wonder that investors in this predicament get sick and tired of holding onto their investment properties and sell up? There is no enjoyment, just costs.

I don't know how to get people to understand the importance of cash flow other than, like Robert Kiyosaki, to keep writing about it. If you can afford to continually take money out of your pocket each week for your investments, that's great. However most people who are on average incomes struggle to afford the luxury of a negative cash flow portfolio.

When I am at social gatherings there will always be one or two people (once they have heard that I am into property investing) who begin to tell me why property investing is a mug's game and how they lost money. They would never do it again and that I am crazy for getting involved in it. Sound familiar? I am sure you have heard the same story or know of someone who sings the 'property is a mug's game' song.

Usually their story goes something like this. They bought their first investment property because a) their friends did, or b) a mate told them to buy that property, or c) a sales agent did a great 'sales' job on them, or d) they felt they needed to 'do something' and bought what they thought was right, or e) it's a hot market and they might miss out... do I need to go on?

These people usually ended up buying their negative cash flow property in a hot market, paying too much for it and/or making the purchase based on emotion rather than facts. So they now have their first investment property and begin thinking they are red-hot property investors until the mortgage payments and expenses start kicking in. What a shock to their system. They keep up the mortgage payments for a while, not realising how much it is eating into their disposable income. They struggle to understand where their money is going each week and start to become more and more frustrated with their cash flow position. They become 'disgruntled landlords' and should the tenant request extra items in the property, such as fly screens, the investor usually reacts negatively no matter how large or small the expense. The tenant becomes unhappy because of the inconvenience and leaves after the tenancy period is up. The property needs cleaning and fixing up prior to the next tenant and this takes about two weeks. It takes a further week to find a new tenant and the investor has to pay the managing agent a at least one week's rent as a letting fee.

The situation goes on for possibly two or three years before the investor decides they have had enough of struggling to keep the property. They decide to sell and find that market conditions have changed, the property is a couple of years older with a little more wear and tear, and they end up selling the property for a loss. If you try to explain to the investor there is a better way, they won't listen as they believe it's not possible.

Let's look at this situation for a moment. The investor buys for all the wrong reasons and struggles to pay for it and has their lifestyle suffer as a result. They finally sell at a loss and all they are left with are bad memories. After a cheap red wine or two they tell every willing listener how bad property investing is, that it's a mug's game, that you are mad for even thinking about it and that you are bound to lose money.

Solution
Don't listen to fallen property investors who drink red wine!

The above typical example highlights the importance of cash flow. Property is a long-term strategy. You won't become rich overnight, you can make a lot of money and some people do. However, property is like good red wine, it needs a few years to mature.

Here's my tip: if you are in a similar situation to the above or you know your investments are sending you broke while you are trying to get rich, then consider adding positive cash flow properties to your portfolio to balance up your negative cash flow. Add properties where the rent pays for the mortgage and expenses, giving you a little extra cash each week that you can use towards sustaining your negative cash flow properties.

The following example shows how positive cash flow properties can balance up negative cash flow properties so an investors' lifestyle is not adversely affected.

Negative cash flow	Positive cash flow

Investment #1
-($140)

Investment #2
+$70

Investment #3
+$35

Investment #4
+$55

Total cost = $70 + $35 + $55 - $140 = $20

If your first investment property is costing you $140 per week out of your pocket, then by adding positive cash flow properties to your portfolio it allows you to pay for the deficit of the negative cash flow property. This means you will not have to dip into your back pocket. Savvy investors always keep their portfolios in balance to ensure their cash flow is in the black rather than in the red.

Speak with your property mentor/coach and seek their expert advice. They can guide you in understanding this concept and how to apply it to your situation. Whatever you do, don't become the person at social gatherings that people try to avoid because you became bitter and twisted over your failure to balance your property portfolio.

Mistake 9 – What's yours is yours – keep it that way

Unless you hear about it at a seminar, speak with like-minded people, read about it in a book or your accountant mentions it, many investors travel their investment journey with no idea about asset protection.

I believe Sydney, Australia is the third highest city in the world for litigation, not far behind New York, USA. How scary is that? You could almost imagine the situation arising whereby looking at a person the wrong way could see you being sued for damages. Litigation is now a reality of life and is the reason that has made asset protection all the more important to us. Structuring your assets correctly could be the difference between being rich and staying rich or being rich and being sued into poverty.

Learn from the rich. They generally place their assets in companies and/or trust structures where they have control of the assets but not ownership. The poor or middle classes generally like all assets to be in their own names, but if they are sued then all assets will be up for grabs.

I worked with a woman some years ago whose husband owned a number of assets including their home in his personal name. When he died, all the assets became part of his estate. Although he had a Will spelling out the disbursement of his assets, his adult children from a previous marriage contested it claiming they were entitled to more than they were allocated.
This woman had to battle it out through the court system and ended up losing her home in order to pay out his children. The

devastation she experienced could have been avoided had they considered the various forms of asset protection available.

Solution

Having a Will myself, I discovered that trusts and the assets within them do not form part of my estate at death. Therefore the beneficiaries of the trust are the only ones entitled to the assets. What I really like about this is that I dictate who my assets go to and not the judicial system.

Even with asset protection just remember that there are three people you cannot protect yourself from:
1) the bank – should you have a mortgage over the property
2) your spouse
3) the tax man

Yet you can generally protect yourself against everyone else by using appropriate structures.

Here's my tip: when considering asset protection speak to qualified asset protection experts but make sure they are also personally experienced at property investing. Ask them lots of questions or buy a book explaining what asset protection is all about. Whatever you do, take asset protection into consideration as part of your investing strategy – it could save you a bundle.

Part 2 – Financials

Mistake 10 – Information overload

This happens to the best of us and it's even worse with 'nervous Nellys'. I have seen 'analysis paralysis' stop investors from buying into fantastic opportunities because they have over-analysed a deal and then talked themselves out of it. The problem here is that fundamentally they do not trust their own judgment, which stops them from moving forward. They have all the great ideas and great information but do nothing with it. Then they spend the rest of their lives living 'in hindsight', complaining of the opportunities they missed out on.

I have clients like this and the biggest challenge I am faced with is reassuring them that their due diligence is correct and that it's time to make the purchase. I must say I do get the biggest buzz when I get them past their analysis paralysis and they purchase an investment property. I often find they become unstoppable once they have mastered moving past their analysis paralysis, and go on to build a portfolio of properties.

A perfect example of this is a client I have who is the best I have seen at research (due diligence). She is almost as good as me! On one of her deals she hesitated to proceed as she felt she had not covered everything and was looking for confirmation of her own due diligence. As always, she over-analysed the area and the numbers, and started to doubt her abilities. Had it not been for my coaching, she would not have proceeded with the deal. Prior to joining my program, she had not purchased any properties for some time because of her analysis paralysis.

Solution

Having a mentor who is an active investor themselves can really help with overcoming analysis paralysis. Find a mentor you can rely on and who will go through the information with you. They must be able to assist and advise if you are on the right path and guide you through any issues as they arise. It is important that they are objective and impartial, otherwise they could add to your paralysis.

Having someone to discuss things with, who has the knowledge and experience to guide you (without doing it for you), will enable you to build your confidence and understanding and make your future property purchases less stressful. My client as a result went on to purchase that property as well as purchase a subsequent property. I have no doubt that understanding her fears as well as building her confidence will lead to her creating a multi-million dollar portfolio in the near future.

Here's my tip: when you find yourself being stopped and unable to move forward, it is usually because you are unsure or have a fear about something (i.e. making a mistake). To overcome this I suggest writing down what it is you are concerned about and endeavor to find a solution to each problem. Fear is usually the biggest obstacle we experience, yet knowledge and action are usually the solution. If you fear making a mistake, it may be because you are missing a piece of information that will help you overcome the fear.

Try using your fear to fuel your quest for knowledge and then take the necessary action to achieve the desired result.

Mistake 11 – Not crunching the numbers properly

The majority of property investors who fail do so because their idea of 'crunching the numbers' is a guestimation of what things will cost without fully understanding the implications of their financial position.

The numbers give an investor a financial understanding of the true cost of an investment, such as whether it is negatively geared, neutral or positive and what the impact will be on their lifestyle. For example, an investor I know purchased a negatively geared property in a major capital city, thinking it would have a shortfall of $100 per week. On proper analysis of the numbers, the investor discovered the property was costing closer to $260 per week (out of pocket). This investor was also wondering why the bank would not lend him more money for further property purchases.

For another example of this, let's revisit the case study mentioned in Mistake 10. The investor who purchased the block of four units discovered that his positive cash flow investment property was actually negative due to the rates and repairs costing more than budgeted.

Solution
When I started out I didn't fully understand the 'power of the numbers' and what that actually meant to me on a weekly basis. It wasn't until my husband and I purchased some analysis software that we could clearly see how much a property would cost us each week and gain a full appreciation of the numbers.

Using the software allowed me to understand how getting into property investing would impact on my lifestyle. It made the numbers 'real' for me.

From then on, before putting in any offers, I would crunch the numbers on each and every property deal. The two variables I played with the most were the purchase price and the rent. If the asking price and the market rent of that property did not meet my requirements I would offer less or increase the rent to see if it changed the bottom line. If the numbers still didn't meet my requirements, even after tweaking, I would walk away and look for something else. My due diligence would let me know what was fair market rent and value for a property.

The software allowed me to play with different scenarios so I could see what I needed to achieve in the purchase price and rent for the deal to stack up. There are a number of software packages on the market that allow you to 'crunch the numbers' on existing and potential property deals. For a small amount of money, software could potentially save you from making a huge financial mistake. Before buying any investment property, I always run the numbers in the software to work out what it will cost me each week. Some analysis software allows you to add in several properties and obtain an overview of the whole portfolio. For example, I looked at a block of units with an excellent rental return. The block of units was on the market for $500,000 and the rental return was approximately $70,000 per year. There were no body corporate fees and there was room to increase the rent. I started to enter the figures into my software. However when I entered in all the costs, including the very high council rates, it made the deal negative. At the time I was looking for cash flow opportunities and had I not crunched the numbers, I would have purchased a block of units that would have cost me around $120 per week.

Here's my tip: crunching the numbers could save you thousands of dollars so if you are going to get into property investing, purchase some quality software as it will be the cheapest asset you buy. Not understanding the rate of return on a property purchase is like gambling and there are too many zeros to get it wrong.

Talk to your mentor/coach for assistance in purchasing the right software for you.

Mistake 12 – Half-baked calculations

Many investors make this mistake. It's because they do not fully understand how to calculate the yield. The fundamental problem is that they do not take into consideration the acquisition, loan and purchase costs of buying property. Let's take a look at some of the additional costs involved:

Acquisition costs
- Deposit
- Planned improvements
- Property finder's fee
- Furniture costs

Purchase costs
- Solicitor's conveyancing costs
- Stamp duty

Loan costs
- Establishment fees
- Mortgagee stamp duty
- Mortgage insurance
- Mortgagee's legal fees
- Valuation fees
- Mortgage registration
- Title registration
- Search fees

As these costs are paid only once, investors sometimes fail to include them when calculating their yield. They often only take into account the property fees such as:

Property expenses
- Rates
- Land lease rates
- Insurance
- Repairs and maintenance
- Body corporate fees
- Pest and building inspections
- Cleaning
- Mowing and garden upkeep
- Letting fees
- Property management fee

As an investor myself, I expect a proper return on my investment (ROI) and the calculation should include all monies spent and received on the investment, not just the ongoing costs of mortgage payments, rates and agent's fees.

Solution

When I calculate the cost of a property purchase, I include all of the abovementioned expenses. I also allow a vacancy period of two weeks per year in case the property is vacant during a tenancy changeover. Many of the costs, such as loan and acquisition-related fees, are a once-off expense. However I do include them in my calculations, as I expect a return on the money spent acquiring the property. The result of not including these costs in your calculations is a false yield.

The idea here is that every dollar you spend should give you a return and by not including these costs in your calculations, your yield will be higher. For example, I knew of an investor who purchased an investment property and placed a 20 per cent deposit on the property. He calculated that the yield would be about 10 per cent, yet when I analysed the numbers with him, he realised it would be less. Here are his figures:

Purchase price:	$300,000
Deposit @ 20%:	$60,000
Loan amount:	$240,000 (approximately)
Weekly rent:	$480

With a loan of $240,000 receiving $480 per week rent he calculated a rental yield of 10 per cent.

You may feel that this is an excellent return to receive but this investor failed to include in his basic calculations the funds for the deposit. The deposit on this occasion was borrowed funds from his line of credit against his own home. There is nothing wrong with borrowing your deposit against your home. However, he is paying interest on that money and yet has not included it in his calculation of rental yield.

Let's do the figures again including the deposit:

Purchase price: $300,000

Deposit @ 20%: $60,000

Loan amount: $300,000 ($240,000 + $60,000 deposit)

Weekly rent: $480 with the opportunity of a rental increase

Actual rental yield is: 8%

Take the rent per week, multiply by 50 weeks (allowing two weeks for vacancy), divide by the purchase price and multiply by 100.

$480 x 50 weeks ÷ $300,000 x 100 = 8%

The above example is a very simplistic calculation of the numbers but what has not been included are all the other costs, listed earlier.

Here's my tip: you need to consider all your costs when calculating your yield. To simplify life, use software that does the hard work for you. There are many software packages on the market so make sure you select software that is reputable and user-friendly. No point having expensive software if you require a masters degree to use it.

It should be noted that most sales agents do not include all costs in their yield calculations.

Mistake 13 – Banks that have a lend of you

There are arguments for and against, however I am a fan of using 'interest-only' loans for investment property purchases. Why? Well, it improves your cash flow by maximising your tax claimable interest and, as cash flow is king, I protect it as if it is gold.

I see many investors with one or even two properties working hard to pay them off. Or they have paid them off and are not leveraging the equity to grow more wealth. These same investors then buy more properties by ill-advisedly securing their own home against their investment properties. This then puts them in the position of possibly losing their own home if something goes horribly wrong with their investment property and they get sued by a tenant.

Let's not kid ourselves here – banks are a business and NOT your friend. They are in business to make money and pay their shareholders a dividend. They are in the business of making a profit from you with as little effort as possible. So why make it easy for them? If I had a dollar for every time I heard an investor tell me how much the bank loves them and all they need to do is pick up the phone and they get what they want, my surname would be TRUMP!

For example, I know of an investor who had one investment property and wanted to purchase a second. The first investment property was fully paid off which means he had considerable equity to use as a deposit on the second property. His bank gave him the loan but wanted the title of the first investment property as security against the second investment property. The investor was happy to do it because the bank kept the interest rate low and it meant he didn't have to do any further work, other than sign the mortgage documents. The risk here was that should something go wrong with the second investment property and the investor is sued by the tenant or visitors of the tenant, it could cost the investor both of the investment properties. This is because the first property is secured against the second.

Solution
Taking out a line of credit on the first investment property, or refinancing and putting the additional equity into a loan offset account and then physically taking out the deposit amount (20 per cent) from the available equity and using it as the deposit on the second investment property is the way I would purchase a second and subsequent properties. I would then borrow the balance (80 per cent) from a lender other than the one who has the loan for the first investment property. The purpose of this is to spread my risk. Should something go wrong with the second investment property, then the first investment property is not at risk. I use many lenders, both traditional and non-traditional, to further spread my risk and as a means of minimising the potential for litigation.

An example of this is as follows:
1st investment property – line of credit to the value of $200,000

Bank 1
Set up line of credit (LOC) and take 20% of the available equity and physically use it as a deposit on the 2nd investment property

2ⁿᵈ investment property

Bank 2
20% deposit from original LOC
Balance of 80% borrowed from Bank 2

Mistake 14 – When it comes to banks, share the love

I regularly hear from investors who think that having an investment home loan, credit card and savings account with the one bank is a good thing. They tell me how their credit card or savings account is fee-free as a result of them having all their accounts with the one bank. They go on to say how easy it is to do internet banking and how great the bank is in assisting them with managing their accounts.

The investor may even obtain additional accounts from the bank for free. The investor believes it is because they're a 'good customer' and they somehow feel privileged to be treated so well from the bank. They may even go further and explain that they have their very own 'personal relationship manger'. Don't they feel special! The unsuspecting investor doesn't realise what is really going on here. Let's think about this situation for a moment. Your investment home loan is usually paid monthly, so the bank can see if you pay your loan on time and whether you pay extra or just the minimum repayment.

Then there are your credit card(s); the bank can see whether you pay the balance off in full each month or just make the minimum repayment. It can see all your spending habits. It can see where you like to shop – Kmart or up market boutiques, it can see how often you fill up the tank with fuel, where you like to dine or where you shop for groceries. Then there is the savings account that most people generally have their paycheck deposited into. So now the bank knows how much you earn each week and how much you have left at the end. It also knows when you receive a pay rise, as your paychecks into the account have increased. It knows if you are a saver or a spender. Now all of a sudden it has a complete picture of your financial spending habits, where you shop, how much you spend, how much you save and how much you pay on your loans.

What happens if something goes wrong (let's say you lose your job) and you decide not to pay off your credit card balance in full this month, like you usually do, and instead you pay the bare minimum to save your pennies until you find another job. You then pay only the interest payment on your investment home loan. Then you may also have difficulty finding another job (or it takes a little while) so there is no regular income going into your savings account as expected.

How much power does the bank have now?

It will notice that your savings account is drying up and you're paying less on your bills. The clauses in your mortgage contract protect the bank and not you as the customer. So should the bank feel a little nervous about your financial position and you miss or default on a payment, no matter how small, it may well decide to call you in on one or all the loans with that particular bank.

Should you fail to meet your payments on the credit card, it may also call you in on your investment home loan. All of a sudden your situation with the bank can become rather unstable and unpleasant. The bank could choose to lower the loan-to-value ratio (LVR) on your investment loans, in which case you may be forced to find significant additional funds to pay the bank for the lower LVR. In short, because it is aware of your financial situation, you are totally exposed. And if it becomes nervous with your temporary financial position, it could sink you overnight.

For example, I know of a builder who had a pregnant wife and young child at home. He wanted to subdivide his home and build two units in his backyard. He obtained approval of a development application (DA) for the units and decided he wanted to build these units himself as an owner-builder. He had ample existing equity and cash, as he had other good investments. As an owner-builder, he needed to stop working to focus on this new project.

All of his accounts were with the one bank. He explained to the bank what his intentions were with regard to building the units. Unfortunately for him, the bank became nervous and decided to issue him with a 30-day notice for him to pay up all his loans or it would repossess his assets, resulting in him and his family being kicked out of their home.

Solution
Spread your risk. How, I hear you ask? The answer is not to put all your eggs in the one basket. What we do is have our credit card(s) with one bank, our savings and everyday working accounts with another bank and our investment home loans are

with several different financiers, both traditional and non-traditional.

We do this so the banks do not know our spending habits unless they go looking. They see that we pay our bills on time and that we are savers. The banks that have our investment loans do not know if I shop at Kmart or up market boutiques. I like the fact that no one bank knows or fully understands our complete financial picture and therefore we can weather a minor storm without being shipwrecked.

Here's my tip: spread your accounts among a number of banks. It makes it a little more difficult for any one bank to have a complete financial history of how you manage your financial affairs. Quite frankly, I can appreciate that banks are only trying to manage their risk but I certainly don't want to help them in a way that may lead to my demise. In fact I can feel quite resentful of banks that use their unilateral power to change a risk rating just because they perceive that the investor may be a higher risk to them. Our personal financial risk mitigation strategy is to apply the above and not put all our eggs in the one basket. Food for thought!

Mistake 15 – Not appreciating depreciation

I have met some successful people along my journey to financial abundance and just recently I met a highly successful, enormously wealthy developer who made his fortune by buying land, developing it and selling it at a sizable profit. He was obviously very good at it because the process that he used was responsible for his significant wealth. His net worth had more zeros than you could poke a stick at. We shared strategies and secrets for wealth creation over a cup of coffee and, to my astonishment, I discovered that he had no idea about depreciation schedules and the tax benefits that could be realised by claiming them against income.

Many investors (regardless of how successful they are) think the best people to calculate tax depreciation benefits are their accountants – WRONG!

If you purchase a new property then you could be missing out on tax benefits if you do not obtain a depreciation schedule from a qualified expert. And the ATO-recognised qualified expert(s) are quantity surveyors, NOT your accountant. Accountants can calculate the allowable depreciation if they know the purchase price of the item, but are generally not qualified to calculate the age or the installation cost of that item, and you could be missing out big time on allowable tax deductions as a result of this.

A quantity surveyor calculates the *installed* value of tax depreciable items in your investment property. The quantity surveyor then produces a tax depreciation schedule. This provides a list of the allowable tax deductions each year over the allowable tax depreciation timeframe. It then breaks these down into two categories – building and chattels (plant and equipment). Your accountant will include the depreciation schedule deductions in your annual tax assessments.

We nearly made this mistake ourselves. We purchased half a dozen properties that were about 30 years old. They had been updated over the years with new carpets, curtains, kitchens and bathrooms. Extensions had been added and walls painted inside and out.

In talking to our quantity surveyor, he advised us that he would have a look at the properties to ascertain if there were any depreciable benefits, even though the properties were old. To our absolute surprise, all depreciation schedules for the six properties came back with generous tax deductible depreciation benefits. We didn't realise all the renovations over the years allowed us to enjoy bigger tax returns.

Solution

If you own a property that has been recently built or is a few years old, or is old but has been renovated, then you could be shortchanging yourself of some serious tax benefits.

When looking for a quantity surveyor, ask your accountant, property manager, other investors or even scour the local phone book or do a web search for suggested names. The cost of getting yourself a depreciation schedule (normally a few hundred dollars) could save you thousands in tax benefits.

For example, I purchased an up market two-bedroom apartment for more than $435,000. Leaving the accountant to produce a tax depreciation schedule would have resulted in most saying that I could only claim around $8000 per year in tax depreciation deductions. However, paying a quantity surveyor around $700 to produce a depreciation schedule legally allowed me to claim a tax benefit of around $17,000 per year for that property. For a few hundred dollars, I was able to enjoy a further $9000 tax benefit which most accountants would have missed. By the way, it is also worthwhile asking your accountant if the cost of producing the depreciation schedule is tax deductible. I think you'll be pleasantly surprised.

If you have an old property that you don't think will attract tax depreciation benefits you may be surprised. Also you may want to research the companies that provide depreciation schedules, as the results can vary greatly. For example, a friend of mine obtained a depreciation schedule on an older property from a local quantity surveyor but was not satisfied with the level of detail in the report. She decided to obtain another schedule from another quantity surveyor who was an investor himself. The difference in tax benefits between the two reports amounted to many thousands of dollars. There are very good quantity surveyors who don't own property but it is a bonus if they do.

Some quantity surveyors offer money-back guarantees if they can't find depreciation benefits equal to twice their fee in the first year of depreciation. I can tell you from my experience it's well worth doing.

Here's my tip: do yourself a favour and don't skimp on this.

Mistake 16 – Hitting the 'financial brick wall'

Wow, I wish I knew about the financial brick wall before we nearly hit it, because it hurt us. Banks don't tell you that they will only lend you a limited amount of money before they see you as a high risk, at which point they put the brakes on your borrowing capacity.

I didn't understand about 'the threshold' and what it meant to cross over it. I had to learn the concept the hard way. It's the bank's internal risk rating that transforms you from being its 'best customer' to some alien from another planet. I don't mean to be harsh on the banks but gee whiz, everything is a secret with the banks until you experience firsthand the wrath of their policies. These policies are written by banks that do not understand wealth creation and generally have an inability to see past their noses. I think I could write a book on this topic alone.

When my husband and I started investing we decided we would try to live off my income (which paid the household bills) and then save my husband's salary to assist with the deposits for purchasing our investment properties. Our jobs paid us well so we were able to pour the savings into purchasing investment properties which we managed to do very well, until one day the banks started to get nervous about lending us any more money. We had nearly hit the proverbial 'brick wall' and we didn't even see it coming. This, by the way, occurred at the time we had purchased our fifth or sixth property. We still had cash flow from our incomes to service more mortgages, but the banks started thinking about turning us away. Just as well we're stubborn and didn't take 'no' for an answer – especially from the banks. We continued to seek out expert advice to try and find a way over this serviceability 'brick wall'.

As it turned out, we hit the jackpot.

Solution

We attended several seminars and read more books on ways to improve our situation. As it turned out, positive cash flow properties were the key to removing the brick wall.

Upon lots of research and analysis of cash flow areas, we purchased six more properties – all giving us approximately a 10 per cent yield. These balanced up our portfolio and freed our borrowing capacity so we could continue buying more and more properties. You don't need to belong to MENSA to buy a negative cash flow property. Any dummy can do it; however, it takes a savvy investor to understand the importance of balancing their portfolio and how to structure it so they can continue growing their wealth.

For example, if you purchase a negative cash flow property that costs you approximately $80 per week to sustain, then consider looking for cash flow positive property(s) that will pay you $80 per week, effectively covering the shortfall from your negative cash flow property. To achieve this, you may even need to purchase two properties earning you $40 per week each. So the idea here is that you constantly keep your portfolio in check by balancing your negative cash flow with your positive cash flow properties. This will help you from hitting the financial brick wall. Cash flow is king in any business, including property. Cash flow is the oil that keeps the investment engine lubricated. Without the oil, the engine seizes up.

Here's my tip: to avoid hitting the financial brick wall, ensure there is enough balanced cash flow in your investment portfolio. This will help to avoid transforming yourself into an alien in the eyes of the banks.

Mistake 17 – Handing in your resignation too soon

I have come across this situation several times now. People have gained a little knowledge about property investing, enjoyed one or two profitable deals and then decided to quit their day job and invest in property full-time. They get 'the bug'. The bug is when they feel they can quit the day job, their only source of regular income, to launch themselves into being a full-time investor.

This is a serious problem, especially if they have no financial backing to launch and sustain themselves into their new chosen career. One or two property transactions or a renovation or two does not make you an expert, and quitting the biggest source of income you have can make the banks extremely nervous.

Just recently a new investor rang to inform me that she'd quit her job to become a full-time investor. It was her intention to buy properties, renovate them and then sell them for a profit. She explained to me that her friend was doing it and is very successful at it. My reaction was that it was great that her friend was doing well but what made her think she would be able to enjoy the same level of success? What would she do if things went wrong? What was her back-up plan? What if there was no profit when she sold? How would she live in the meantime? How would she be able to sustain the mortgage if the property didn't sell when she needed it to? Did she realise she would be relegated to higher interest 'low doc' and/or 'no doc' loan products, and not the low interest 'full doc' loans she had attracted when she was employed? What was her exit strategy for these scenarios?

To add to this picture, banks generally lend less money, or at higher interest rates, to people who are self-employed compared to those who work for a boss. The banks are all about making a profit with minimal risk and the one thing banks love are that their customers receive regular paychecks from their employers. They see people with day jobs as a being a lower risk than self-employed people and will therefore lend them more and at lower rates. A 'full doc' borrower can obtain up to 100 per cent for an investment loan, whereas a 'low doc' borrower can traditionally only borrow up to 80 per cent. Therefore the investor needs to find a higher deposit amount to secure the finance compared to a 'full doc' borrower.

Can you imagine this woman going into the bank wanting to borrow money for an investment property? She may secure finance for one property (I'll be generous and assume they give her finance for two properties), but what happens after that? To become a full-time investor, I would imagine that you would want to do more than two deals. What do you do with the rest of your time?

Solution
It's great to have a dream and follow your passion but it is also important to plan for it. Throwing in your primary source of income can be financially irresponsible.

Here's my tip: it's important to plan your future. If you want to become a full-time investor, set up a strategy for how you are going to do this.

Ed and I had set up a five-year plan whereby we would focus our energy and funds on buying as many properties as we could. We also analysed the portfolio to ensure it was balanced and gave us an overall cash surplus.

Our intention was for us to run our property investment business part-time while working in full-time employment, until it allowed us the opportunity to step out of the rat race and enjoy the lifestyle we desire.

Part 3 – Purchasing

Mistake 18 – No money down – too good to be true?

Yes they do exist, they actually do. We would not have accumulated as many properties as we have had we not been able to apply 'no money down' strategies. However I do get the odd cynic who doesn't believe it's possible and usually it's due to the fact that they are unclear or have not applied 'no money down deal' strategies.

Rather than focus on the mistake, let me go straight to the solution where I will give you a number of ways to structure 'no money down deals'. I might even provoke some thought and give you ideas on how else you can do them.

Solution

There are a number of ways to do 'no money down deals'. It's all about thinking outside the square. You may require some cash at some point for unexpected expenses, however the concept is that you get your money back by the time the deal is done and dusted. Therefore a 'no money down deal' means you are not contributing any of your personal cash into the overall deal.

Here are five possible scenarios for doing 'no money down deals':
1. Existing equity
2. Revolving credit
3. Delayed settlement with renovation
4. Long term settlement – off the plan
5. Equity partner
1. Existing equity

Many people have their own homes or are paying off a mortgage. The concept here is to use the equity in your home to purchase investment properties. For example, to purchase a property you need a deposit. Let's say the deposit required is 20 per cent. The idea is that you take the available equity in your home and use it as a deposit to secure the new investment property. You then borrow the remaining 80 per cent from another bank.

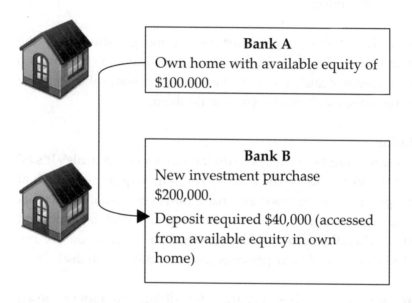

Bank A
Own home with available equity of $100.000.

Bank B
New investment purchase $200,000.

Deposit required $40,000 (accessed from available equity in own home)

2.   Revolving credit

A revolving line of credit (LOC) works best when you have your own personal property paid off or nearly paid off. The principal here is that you refinance the loan on your property and obtain a LOC against the available equity in the property. Armed with the cash from this LOC, you are an attractive buyer for most sellers because you are able to offer unconditional and/or short settlement terms. This in turn should enable you to negotiate a significant discount when purchasing your next investment property, especially if the seller is 'distressed'. The discounted purchase price should be at least equal to 90 per cent of the market value of the property; the idea here being that eight weeks after cash settlement of the property, you can then take out finance on the new property which will then release a LOC for you to repeat the same purchasing process on another investment property. For example, let's assume that your LOC was $300,000 and you were able to purchase a new investment property with a market value of $330,000, at a discounted price of $300,000. Eight weeks after cash settlement of the new property you would then be able to apply for finance on the new property. The bank valuer would value the property at market value ($330,000) and the bank would provide you with a LOC on the new property of $300,000 at a 90% LVR. This means that subject to the bank's lending constraints, you could effectively buy a new investment property every eight weeks using the original $300,000 as a revolving LOC and not have to use any of your own money for deposits because the deposit amount equates to your discount amount on each property.

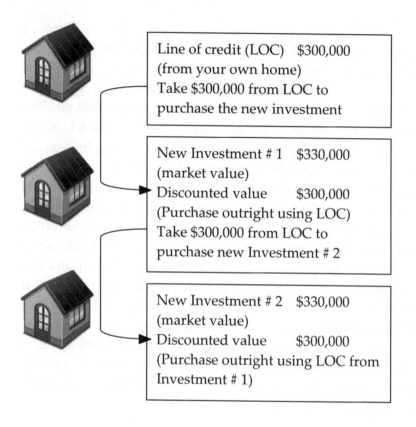

Line of credit (LOC) $300,000
(from your own home)
Take $300,000 from LOC to
purchase the new investment

New Investment # 1 $330,000
(market value)
Discounted value $300,000
(Purchase outright using LOC)
Take $300,000 from LOC to
purchase new Investment # 2

New Investment # 2 $330,000
(market value)
Discounted value $300,000
(Purchase outright using LOC from
Investment # 1)

3.   Delayed settlement with renovation

This strategy can be very successful but you need to be careful to ensure that the improvements you make to the property will increase its value. Purchase a property below market value and secure a three to six month delayed settlement. Tidy the property up and commission an independent valuation four weeks prior to settlement. Then take a mortgage on the property for 80 per cent of the independent valuation. If your financial position is such that you could borrow up to 90 per cent, then you could use the excess to purchase another property.

For example, a property is on the market for $200,000. You negotiate a longer settlement with the ability to access the property prior to settlement to enable you to conduct your renovation. You have also negotiated a discount, paying only $160,000. Your renovation costs are $30,000. Prior to settlement, you obtain a valuation for the property. Due to the value you added, the valuation is now $250,000, an increase of $90,000 on your purchase price or $60,000 after your renovation expenses are taken out. Buying below market and adding value has allowed you to create a 'no money down deal'.

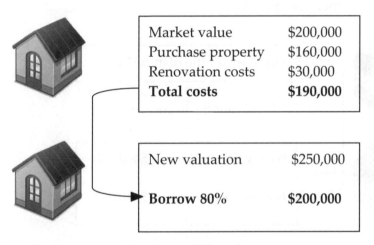

Market value	$200,000
Purchase property	$160,000
Renovation costs	$30,000
Total costs	**$190,000**

New valuation	$250,000
Borrow 80%	**$200,000**

4.   Long-term settlement – off the plan

This is when you buy off the plan and have a one to two-year settlement period. Usually the deposit you provide is very small. To avoid using cash, you could obtain a bank guarantee or deposit bond instead. The development takes a long time to build, during which time the property goes up in value. At the time of settlement (as it's at least 12 months since you purchased it), you can request that the valuation be done on the new market value and not your contract price. (<u>Note</u> – you would only want to do this if you are sure that the value has increased).

You can then borrow against the value of the new price, which is greater than the contract price. For example, you purchase a townhouse off the plan for $340,000. It takes more than 12 months to build. The market has gone up by the time you come to settle the property, putting the new valuation price at $400,000. You borrow 80 per cent of $400,000 which is your purchase price of $340,000. If you are in the position to borrow up to 90 per cent, then you could borrow the $360,000 and use the excess funds to purchase another investment.

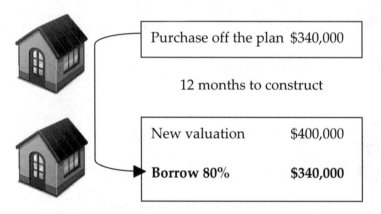

Purchase off the plan $340,000	
12 months to construct	
New valuation	$400,000
Borrow 80%	**$340,000**

5. Equity partner

This is how we purchased two of our properties. We found an equity partner who wanted to invest but lacked the borrowing capacity, whereas we had borrowing capacity and lacked equity. They put in the deposit plus costs and we borrowed the balance from the bank. It was a perfect arrangement, so much so we did it again. The terms of the joint venture agreement can be whatever you need them to be. You are only limited by your imagination.

As long as you have the right intentions then the transaction can be very successful and lucrative for both parties.

Here's my tip: when using an equity partner, make sure you are clear up front what your exit strategy will be. You need to know if your partner is happy to hold onto the property for a number of years or whether they want out of the deal in 12 months. Also set up some rules around one party needing to sell and how you manage that. You will need to obtain professional advice from a solicitor.

Mistake 19 – Hanging onto a sinking ship

This usually happens when an investor is emotionally attached to buying a property. I see it all the time. There is such a desperation to make the deal work, and almost at any cost, that they lose perceptive.

I have seen many investors source a property they want to buy, research the area, speak to all the relevant people such as councils, finance brokers, real estate agents and property managers and then they crunch the numbers. They find out that the numbers do not stack up so they go to great lengths to make the deal work because they have become emotionally attached to the outcome.

I had a client who did this with an off-the-plan house-and-land package. The particular area she was researching offered turnkey packages for around $370,000 plus. In addition to this, stamp duty, plants for the garden and a reticulation system needed to be added to the price. The other issue was that there was very little difference in the cost of building a three or four-bedroom house. (You may not think this is a problem, however in this case it was because every house in the estate had four bedrooms, thus making them all identical). This investor was so keen to buy in the area, but while she was looking into it the cost of housing continued to climb.

She set about researching all the builders in the area to see if she could purchase a house-and-land package within her price range. She looked at smaller blocks of land with larger houses and larger blocks with smaller houses, however every variation continued to be too expensive. This investor eventually let go of the sinking ship and moved on to look at other areas with homes that were more affordable yet offering a similar rental return. I have seen other investors continue to negotiate in the hope of finding the right deal. Unfortunately, on an emotional level, this experience can lead to investors not pursuing other deals altogether. They are stopped dead in their tracks and struggle to get back into the market, as they feel they will fail to negotiate a great deal for themselves.

Solution
It is easier said than done, especially if you are a new investor. It is important not to get emotional about purchasing an investment property.

Here's my tip: use the numbers as the 'bad cop' and make yourself the 'good cop'. What I mean by that is when a sales agent tells you your offer is too low, you explain to them that your numbers specifically tell you that you cannot afford anything higher than your offer. Also explain that should you increase your offer, you could risk financial hardship.

Advise the agent that you want the vendor to get a good deal and that you want a good deal for yourself as well – we call this a 'win-win'. The numbers are a good excuse for moving on should the deal not work out and the real benefit is that it stops you from continuing to negotiate when you are in a weak position.

For example, some years ago I found an opportunity in which a vendor was offering land for development. He offered settlement of the land to occur when the units were sold and settled with the buyers. I was very excited at being able to develop 15 units in a fantastic location, in an up and coming area with huge potential. I was very attached to this deal due to the vendor being a lovely old man who wanted to work with me to make the deal work. I also knew that the profit was exceptional, provided all the units were able to be sold at the required selling price. I worked hard to conduct all the necessary due diligence and even commissioned an architect to review the site. I spoke to the council on numerous occasions as it was in favor of what I wanted to achieve with this site. The location was perfect for the development I had in mind. With all that support it made it hard to let go of this sinking ship.

The problem I faced was that the selling price could not be validated. Real estate agents in the area could not provide comparable sales equivalent to what would be built and therefore the selling price was estimated. The numbers and the lack of relevant data caused us to let go of this sinking ship. As hard as it was, it proved to be the best decision for us at the time. Looking back, it would have been an emotional decision and financially we would have suffered had we proceeded with the deal.

Mistake 20 – I have to have it

This is a classic mistake. Many investors get so caught up in the emotion of buying a property that they lose sight of what it's really worth. I have seen it many times at auctions. You can always tell the savvy investors as they strategically place their bids and stop when they have reached their limit. The novice buyers have emotion invested in each bid and they forget to stop. Emotion is the key factor to bad buys at auctions, which by their very nature put the seller and buyer under pressure. The concept of an auction is to have a winner and society teaches us that 'winning' is a good thing. At an auction it becomes dangerous.

Here's my tip: have a level head at auctions by using the 'numbers' generated from your financial calculations.

At a seminar I went to, I met a guy who had purchased a property in another state while on holidays. This was before he had an education in property investing. Unfortunately, his lack of understanding cost him dearly as he was still paying for it some years later. He was unsuspectingly convinced to purchase a house that was priced $50,000 more than it was worth. It wasn't until he purchased the property and tried to revalue it some time after that he realised what had happened. He had borrowed the maximum amount from the bank and would have made a huge loss if he had been forced to sell it, one he definitely couldn't afford. His solution was to keep the property until it eventually grew in capital growth, allowing him to sell without incurring any losses. It is a sad case but it does happen to people who travel on holidays, enjoy the area they are in and then decide to purchase an investment property there. They fail to undertake any due diligence and they do not understand the area. This more often than not is a recipe for disaster.

Solution

Controlling your emotions is the key. A way to prevent paying too much for a property is to look for similar properties that have recently sold and how much they sold for. This will give you an indication of how much you should be paying for yours.

Even if you are on holidays and insist on buying something, before you buy have a look at other properties being sold by real estate agents in the area. Look at as many properties as possible. This will give you a better understanding of what properties are selling for in the area and what you should or shouldn't be paying for yours.

Here's my tip: be very careful while on holidays to not get caught up in the emotion of the wonderful location you are staying in. Often holiday destinations are seasonal, which means the property can remain vacant for long periods during the off season. Do not sign anything unless you have sought professional advice from independent experts.

To prevent paying too much for a property, it helps to put your initial offer in at a lower than market value price. Go into negotiations offering less than what the vendor is asking for, for example, as a rule I always start my negotiations by offering at least 20 per cent less than the asking price. Now I can hear some of you cringing at this suggestion. Remember that the worst that can happen is they say 'no'. Negotiating is all about confidence. The more knowledge and experience you have, the more confident you will feel about making a low offer. I find the psychology of negotiating rather interesting. It stems from our childhood. As children we are raised in an environment where we are always told 'no' and so as adults we are afraid of asking in fear of getting a 'no' response. For example, as a child you may ask:

"mum, can I have another lolly?" – NO, you have had enough!
"mum, can I stay up a little longer?" – NO, it's already past your bedtime.
"mum, can I stay home from school today?" – NO, you are not sick.
"dad, can I watch TV?" – NO, finish your homework first.
"dad, can I have a horse for Christmas?" – NO, we can't afford it.

As adults, we fail to ask for the pay rise we deserve because we have already determined in our minds that the boss will say 'no'. As adults, we fail to ask for discounts when making purchases in the fear we will be rejected, and we all resent being rejected.

The negative response during negotiations is not a personal rejection of you, it's our upbringing that makes us believe that it is. We feel bad for asking for something we want and so we fail to negotiate the best deal for ourselves time and time again. If you learn to ask more often, I believe you could save yourself around 20 per cent of your income – amazing when you think about it.

When I was working in the corporate world, I was doing the job of two people. Having had enough of doing that and not being appreciated or rewarded for it, I arranged a meeting to see the boss. In that meeting I explained the situation, that I had had enough and things needed to change. His response was "how do we make it work?" Just from that conversation and asking for what I wanted, I ended up with a huge increase in job satisfaction, a company vehicle, and recognition for my efforts by my peers and management. I had a fresh focus and a new commitment to making a success of my new position. Had I not asked for what I wanted, I would have continued to complain to others, gossip, be negative, resentful, isolated and very unproductive. My job dissatisfaction would have continued and resulted in my eventual resignation.

Here's my tip: never be afraid to ask for what you want. The worst that can happen is a 'no'. If you are prepared for the 'no' then everything else is a bonus.

For everyone reading this book, please, please, please do yourselves a favour and always try to negotiate yourselves a better deal by asking for less when buying and more when selling.

Mistake 21 – Investing in a lemon

It's a tragedy when investors do not consider what the market wants when they buy investment properties. They then wonder why they do not get the rent they are seeking.

A friend of mine looked at purchasing a unit in a highly sought after area in which she thought any unit would be appropriate for tenants. However, to her surprise, after interviewing several property managers in that specific area, she discovered that two-bedroom apartments with balconies rented quickly. Had she settled for just any unit, the consequences could have been a longer period of vacancy and/or lower rent.

The same could be said for purchasing properties in an area where mostly retirees reside. I have seen investors purchase properties that are on the second floor of a building with no easy access lifts, or they build new properties that are multi-level. What they have not considered is that retirees generally prefer not to have to climb stairs. Their preference is for single-level buildings or buildings with lifts. That's not to say these properties will not rent. However, you can see how you can mistakenly limit your potential market by making the wrong investment choice. For example, when we purchased our own home it was our intention to renovate it to sell and then move on. We selected this property as it had potential for improvement. It was also the type of property that is highly desirable to most people wanting to live in the area.

We had designers and architects come through and give us ideas and quotes for the renovation. The most commonly asked question by them was 'why don't you extend up?' Our response was that if we were to extend up we would be overcapitalising for the market we wished to sell into. We didn't want to build a 'Taj Mahal' as it would have limited our market when selling. Even if we decided to keep the property and rent it out, building the Taj Mahal would not have earned us any more rental income.

Solution
Just remember, you are trying to buy what your prospective tenants want and not what you want. We often hear how seaside towns or suburbs are appealing to people. As investors we think purchasing property with water views can be very lucrative. The

downside to this type of investment is that they may be expensive to purchase and they may not attract the rental return required to make the numbers stack up. That's not to say that waterfront properties are not what the market wants or likes. Just make sure you consider what tenants want and what they are prepared to pay for.

Unless you have some cash flow or equity to support such a property, it can be very costly to sustain. I know an investor who purchased a $2 million waterfront property with an old house on it with the intention of building his dream home one day. When purchasing this property he realised the rent he would receive would be minimal, so he had to structure his finances to sustain the mortgage until the day came when he was ready to build. I might add that this investor had several other investment properties with a cash flow surplus that allowed him to purchase this waterfront property. For a new investor, or an investor with only a couple of investments, it may be better to stick with investments that are around the median price and rent levels. Once you have built your portfolio, getting into deals that are more lifestyle orientated becomes easier to sustain over the longer term. Best to have a solid foundation built before you launch into buying your multi-million dollar dream home.

Here's my tip: always keep in mind what the majority of people are looking for when you buy your investment properties. The more people who are after your property, the easier it will be to rent or sell.

Mistake 22 – Not buying time when buying a property

This is a common mistake made by investors and one I regularly see with my clients. It doesn't take long for them to get sick and tired of missing out on deals before they finally learn that they need to get the property off the market so they can do their due diligence without being under pressure from other buyers.

There is nothing worse than trying to buy property and being gazumped by another buyer each time. I too have made this mistake and it is why I insist that my investor clients take the property off the market so they can undertake further due diligence without pressure from other buyers. I hated it when I saw a property I wanted to buy, did the necessary research and put in an offer, only to be told it was already sold. I wasted many hours researching deals that I'd miss out on time and time again, especially in a hot market.

One particular client of mine has also fallen prey to this situation. He continued to miss out on opportunities in the hope of conducting due diligence first, even though I had repeatedly explained to him that getting the property off the market in the first instance was critical. He finally listened and started taking property off the market in order to buy himself some time to organise his inspections, reports, etc. Frustration had become the catalyst for taking the property off the market. As he knew the area exceptionally well, I had no doubt his due diligence would be detailed.

Solution
The key to taking a property off the market is to put in an offer and include contract clauses that make the contract conditional upon you undertaking certain searches and due diligence. Using

Special Conditions contract clauses allows you to take the property off the market so you can conduct your due diligence before unconditionally having to commit to purchasing the property. The clauses you use (I prefer clauses written by a solicitor) will allow you to withdraw from the deal should your research uncover anything unfavourable.

As an investor what you want is time and taking the property off the market while conducting your due diligence is what savvy investors do. For example, when purchasing property, I always use a 'due diligence' clause with a period of about 35 days. This clause allows me to conduct all my research in a timely manner whereby I am not under pressure, especially if I am purchasing property in another state.

By using this clause I am able to secure the property and prevent others bidding on it for those 35 days. It's an ideal way to purchase property. Why would anyone want to purchase under pressure when you may not have all your facts, therefore increasing your risk of making a mistake? Taking the property off the market buys you the time you need to ensure your investment is a great one.

Here's my tip: ensure you seek legal advice for the content of your 'subject to' clauses before including them in a contract of sale.

Mistake 23 – The fine print

Most investors I have spoken to do not understand what I mean by this. Most happily sign contract agreements to purchase property without fully comprehending what they are signing up for and when things go horribly wrong, they'll cry foul and blame everyone else. At the end of the day, you and you alone are accountable for making sure you have the right clauses in your purchase contracts. You should, of course, consult with your solicitor before signing any purchase contract.

Not having the right clauses in purchase contracts can be particularly disastrous for investors who are unaware of the potential dangers of buying property from unscrupulous property marketing companies that prey on unsuspecting, inexperienced and uneducated investors. Generally, contracts for purchasing property are now standard documents that have been developed by reputable organisations such as the Real Estate Institute in each state. There is provision in most purchase contracts to add Special Condition clauses that allow you, as the buyer, to include buying conditions that will protect you and your particular interests. Note that it is extremely important that you consult with your solicitor before signing any contract to purchase property. This includes any Special Condition clauses that you may wish to insert in the contract.

Below is an example of a contract clause taken directly from a contract of sale that we received when purchasing one of our investment properties. The special condition clause in this contract was added by the vendor and, on the face of it, allowed us as the buyer to conduct a building inspection on the property before settlement and pull out of the deal if there were structural defects. You would think this was a good clause to have, however take a closer look at the wording of the clause:

"In relation to the building inspection report, such report may only be deemed to be unsatisfactory to the buyer if the report identifies structural defects in the dwelling."

Note that in the above clause it stipulates that 'structural defects' are the only grounds for pulling out of the contract. This means that as long as there are four walls and a roof and the place isn't falling down, it would be difficult to withdraw from this contract. What would happen if the owners of the property frequently held parties during which all doors, windows and walls were damaged? Under the wording of this clause, you would not be able to withdraw from the contract, even if it was going to cost thousands of dollars to repair the damage.

Remember, make sure you seek legal advice from a registered solicitor before signing any contract. I know of an investor who had this very thing happen to him. He tried to get out of the deal but it was too late and he was locked in. To prevent losing his deposit, the way forward was to go back to the vendor and renegotiate the purchase price. Luckily in this case, the vendor compensated the investor for the damage. He did this by lowering the purchase price to cover the cost of repairs. The vendor didn't have to do this though and the investor could have been up for a lot of money to fix the damage.

Solution
Use Special Condition clauses that protect you as the investor. For example, the clause below is a building inspection clause that we use to cover us for any building issues. It is written in such a way that it protects us, the investor;
"This contract is subject to the buyer and/or the buyers' nominated registered builder being satisfied with the results of a building

inspection of the building within 10 days from the date of this contract, failing which this contract will be at an end, the deposit refunded to the buyer and neither party will have any claim against the other apart from any rights either of the parties may have against the other as a result of any breach of this contract."

Can you see the difference? Remember to always obtain legal advice on the wording of any contract and any contract clauses that you wish to include.

Here's my tip: I would not purchase an investment property unless I had included Special Condition clauses that protected my interests as the buyer. If a vendor refused to allow me to insert these clauses, I would walk away from the deal.

Mistake 24 – Buying low demand properties

You can make money from all types of properties, including holiday homes and granny flats. However low demand properties can become a high risk in a down market.

Low demand properties are usually properties that only appeal to a small segment of the market, so if you need to sell the property there will be a limited number of people wanting to buy it from you. Examples of low demand properties are student accommodation, serviced apartments and retirement villages, which, for the new investor, carry a certain amount of risk (some people will disagree with me on this and that's okay). The problem with student accommodation is that it is usually custom built to the needs of students. This type of property usually provides the investor with a reasonable return on their investment, however when it comes to selling the property, you can really only sell it to another investor who wants to buy student accommodation, which really limits your available selling market. This constraint is generally reflected in poor capital growth for this type of property.

I had a client who purchased an apartment in a building that was custom built for student accommodation. He bought it before he knew me and thought he had made a great purchase, however on further analysis he could see that what he had purchased was not really a good deal. The reason being that it was negatively geared with very little capital growth – around 3 to 5 per cent per annum. This is fairly typical for these specialised investments. Had he purchased a normal one-bedroom apartment not tailored for students in the same suburb, history showed he would have enjoyed an average capital growth rate of 10 per cent over the past 10 years.

The same can be said about retirement village accommodation. Traditionally this type of accommodation consists of very small one-bedroom units that are part of a larger community development. The thing against buying this type of property is that you can only sell it to retirees who usually don't have a lot of money to spend on accommodation. This then tends to 'cap' capital growth levels for this type of property.

The other problem with low demand properties is getting finance. Banks typically lower the LVR (loan-to-value ratio) which means you need to put in a larger deposit, sometimes up to 40 per cent. This is an indication that even the banks see this type of investment as high risk.

Solution

Buying low demand properties comes with higher risk and unless you are prepared to put your hand in your pocket to sustain them, they can limit your financial capacity to borrow and grow your wealth. Look for high demand properties such as houses or units that have appeal to the greater rental and seller market. For example, one of our investment properties is a one-bedroom apartment in a sought after location, close to transport, shops, restaurants and within easy access of the city and universities. What is great about this property is that we could easily rent it out to a student, a single person or a couple. This ensures our property is desirable to many groups of tenants. The same would apply should we choose to sell the property. Having this sort of investment lowers our risk as it appeals to owner-occupiers and investors alike. All of a sudden you open yourself up to a wider market and increase your probabilities of selling sooner rather than later.

Here's my tip: whatever you decide to do, keep your options open as this will help you when looking to lease or sell your property. The key is to have as many people wanting to rent or buy your property as possible. This helps to secure the future of your investment.

Mistake 25 – The low points of high-rise

You can make money buying 'off the plan' in high-rise apartments, but doing so can attract its own level of risk which should not be ignored. What I mean by this is that high-rise apartment blocks may have lovely views and fantastic locations, but can attract their own problems. For instance:

• the banks assess them differently from a lending perspective,
• property values can fail to grow, or in many cases even drop in value,
• body corporate fees are generally high, and
• rents can fluctuate depending on the volume of apartments in the building.

I have talked to many investors purchasing apartments 'off the plan' in multi-level high-rise apartment blocks using a 'bank guarantee' or a 'deposit bond' to secure the property. The development usually takes two to three years to build and grow in value, even though the investor hasn't settled the property. The intention of the investor is that by the time it comes to settling the property, it will have significantly grown in value and the investor will try to borrow using the end value of the property and not the purchase price. This strategy is a gamble and I have seen investors pay a heavy price for following it. I have even heard of investors who have lost their own homes as a result of adopting this strategy. I'm not suggesting that people shouldn't use it, just that they should be careful when using it.

A friend of mine had a relative who, during a boom in the property market, purchased two investment properties in a high-rise apartment block. The purchase price of these apartments was $650,000 each. He paid a small deposit to secure these purchases with the intention of using the capital growth in the properties to pay for the balance of the deposit when the properties settled. The apartments took two years to construct, during which time the market dropped and the banks became very nervous about his over exposure.

So for this investor it was a double whammy. The price of the apartments fell considerably and the banks would only lend him 70 per cent of the valuation.

Diagram 1 – this is what the investor thought would happen when the property settled two years later.
Purchase price: $650,000
New bank valuation price: $780,000
Bank LVR (90%):   **$702,000**

Diagram 2 – this is what actually happened two years later.
Purchase price: $650,000
New bank valuation price: $580,000
Bank LVR (70%): $406,000

Therefore this investor needed to find an additional $244,000 per property (totaling $488,000) to be able to settle his purchases. The risk with high-rise apartments is not only the market fluctuation but also when property values go down banks get nervous and can change the LVR. The lowering of LVR was more detrimental to this investor than the property value going down.

The other problem with buying high-rise apartments is that you are one of hundreds of owners within the apartment block and if an owner doesn't have the funds to settle the property, he becomes a desperate seller and will need to sell quickly. When he can't sell the property because he is asking for above market value for the property, he has no option but to drop his price. When he does and it sells, this price then becomes the new benchmark price for all other apartments in the high-rise block of apartments. If your property is similar in size and features, then unfortunately your property will be devalued as well.

Solution

Buying in high-rise apartment developments is a completely different ball game to buying a house or a unit in the suburbs. It can have some advantages (such as long term settlements and the use of smaller deposits), however if capital growth does not occur, it can leave you in a very precarious situation. Unless you are skilled in the game of buying apartments in high-rise apartment developments, my suggestion is to stick to developments of 20 units or less, located in the suburbs.

If you choose to go down the path of buying in large developments as we have done, just make sure you have a back-up plan should things go wrong. Our exit strategy when buying an apartment off the plan is to keep some equity aside to assist with the deposit should the value drop or the banks lower their LVR. There would be nothing more stressful than having to lose a deposit or end up in financial hardship due to the market changing and catching you unaware.

Here's my tip: if you are going to buy in high-rise apartment blocks, then it is really important you do two things.
1) Do your research and make sure you purchase with the tenant in mind, as this will assist you in deciding whether to buy a one, two or three-bedroom apartment.
2) Have an exit strategy so you can manage your financial affairs should things go wrong.

Mistake 26 – Size does matter

No-one will tell you this until you try to get finance, but if the property you are buying is too small in size, obtaining finance becomes more difficult as the banks see it as high risk.

Similarly to Mistake 24, banks see properties that are too small as specialised and therefore a risk. For example, it is generally difficult to sell serviced apartments or hotel rooms. You couldn't sell a hotel room to an owner-occupier to live in – unless you are Donald Trump and own the whole building. As that is probably not the case, selling the property would have to be to another investor.

Occupancy rates for hotel rooms and serviced apartments are generally around 70 per cent. What that means is the investment (hotel room) is occupied for 70 per cent of the year, leaving a shortfall of 30 per cent. Plus there are body corporate fees that must be paid for the maintenance and upkeep of the property. In addition to this, there is also a sinking fund which the company managing the complex uses to refurbish the hotel every five or so years.

I know someone who owns a double-storey residential block of one-bedroom flats. He leases the units out to single people only, as the units are about 32 sqm in size (or 4 squares). When he went to the bank wanting to revalue the block of units so he could access some of the equity, the bank would only lend him 60 per cent of the new valuation, citing the size of the units as the reason for not lending him any more. This limited his ability to buy more investment properties.

Solution

I understand some investors will want to purchase a small sized investment property just so they can get into the market, however if purchasing the property limits your wealth creating capacity, then you may be better off finding a joint venture partner and purchasing a larger property. For example, if your deposit is too small to purchase anything larger with, then consider a joint venture partner who could contribute and increase the overall deposit. Your combined borrowing power may also allow you to borrow more and purchase a better returning investment property.

Here's my tip: seek expert advice from your accountant and solicitor as to whether joint ventures are a good buying strategy for you.

Our philosophy when it comes to joint ventures is that we would rather own 50 per cent of a great performing property than 100 per cent of nothing or an under-performing property. Buying a property in a joint venture can give you the ability to leverage more from the investment than if you purchased a smaller non-performing property on your own.

If you want to purchase an investment property on your own, consider its size. For example, an investor I know purchased a studio apartment that was small. She struggled to obtain finance for it and the end result was an LVR of 70 per cent. Had the apartment been 20 sqm larger the LVR would have been greater. Our one-bedroom apartment is 78 sqm in size and we were able to borrow 90 per cent from the banks. We would rather borrow more and use our deposit to purchase two properties than pour all our money into a deposit for one property.

Mistake 27 – Investing in high-risk areas

We have invested in high-risk areas, successfully and unsuccessfully. There is sometimes an element of speculation in the opportunity, but it's the exit strategy that can soften the blow if things don't go according to plan. For example, about four years ago we found an area to invest in that had positive cash flow properties and was experiencing high capital growth. It was a double bonus – every investor's dream. We went on to purchase several properties there that have made a sizeable contribution to our overall net wealth. This area, however, depends on one industry, which equates to high risk. By this I mean that if something goes wrong with the industry or the economics of that one industry, it can have a devastating effect on the community, which in turn would flow on to include any investments in the town. Because we conducted a lot of research into the town and the industry that supported it, all has gone very well and looks good for the foreseeable future.

In another part of the country we speculated and bought a property in another small town with a much smaller population in a high-risk area. It had the relevant infrastructure required to sustain it, including a multi-million dollar upgrade to the local hospital. Again, there was only one major industry. We purchased a block of land with the intention of building units on it. However what we did not consider at the time were the weather patterns. The area has recently suffered from drought conditions that caused many people to stop spending. Fortunately for us we were able to sustain the expense of holding onto the block of land but I know of people who have struggled. This scenario demonstrates that investing in high risk areas can be costly, even if you have covered all your bases.

Another example of the impact of purchasing in high-risk areas comes to mind. A person I know told me about a great waterfront block of raw land that he purchased years ago for the bargain price of $10,000. His friend at the time told him it would be a great buy for the future. The block of land was on an island accessible only by boat. There was a small number of permanent residents living on the island and it was known as a holiday destination for backpackers and campers.

His dream investment for the future turned out to be a nightmare. He was aware the block did not have any utilities such as water, gas, sewerage, storm water and electricity services connected to it but didn't realise or appreciate the high cost of installing and connecting these services. It also turned out that the land was overpriced when compared to recent similar land purchases. The council rates over the years he owned it added up to more than the original cost of the land and in order to build his dream home on the island he would have had to ship all the necessary materials, equipment and machinery across the water. This made the cost of building his house a very expensive exercise.

Solution
Develop an exit strategy for the 'what if' scenario of any high-risk purchase and stick to it. Identify all known risks and draw up a plan of how you are going to manage and mitigate them. It's absolutely imperative that you think ahead when purchasing property. We usually work in reverse when purchasing our investment properties. We start by identifying all the things that can potentially go wrong with the property and if we can't mitigate each risk to low then we don't proceed.

Purchasing property in rural towns with single industries such as mining, agriculture and tourism will require a lot more research and risk mitigation than purchases in major capital cities. For example, if you chose to buy in an area where mining is the main source of employment in the town, try to consider the probability and long-term impact on the town if that industry were to shut down. In order to determine this and to develop mitigation and exit strategies for the 'what if' scenario, look at the relevant company and government websites. Talk to local councils and government bodies for insights into how long the industry is likely to last. Also consider the macro economy of the industry to ascertain its future demand and impact on the global markets. If demand for what is being produced is high or increasing, then this can be a good sign. You might want to look at the life cycle of the industry, as history can often be a good guide to predicting the future.

Should agriculture be the main source of employment for the town, then consider the weather patterns and the sort of produce that is being grown. Have a look at long-term demand and try to foresee any issues that may arise in the future. When we purchased our block of land in a small rural town, I certainly didn't consider the weather to be a risk, so don't make my mistake and make sure you consider this when making your purchasing decisions.

As for tourism, well the world didn't plan for the Bali bombing, bird flu, September 11 or the tsunami to happen. When tourism is the main industry and source of employment in a town or city, then the impact on these communities can be devastating. This can include the impact on property prices. Therefore it is really important when purchasing investment property to take into consideration your risk mitigation and exit strategies. Questions like:

• What will you do should tourism in the town dry up?
• What will happen to my investment in that town or area?
• How should I deal with the problem?
• What will my exit strategy be so that I minimise my loss?

Here's my tip: I don't want to scare off any investor from purchasing property in high-risk areas, as there is definitely money to be made in these places, just consider all your risks and ensure you have a back-up plan and exit strategy You'll sleep better at night if you do.

Mistake 28 – Buying sight unseen

Buying sight unseen is a fabulous way to buy real estate; unfortunately many investors get it wrong. I once listened to a property guru who, while on stage, mentioned that in his opinion new investors should not buy property sight unseen until they have at least viewed 100 properties. I happen to agree. I can't tell you how many properties I have viewed over the years. For months on end it was all Ed and I did every weekend. We used to get up early every Saturday morning and head straight to the real estate agent's office so we could view as many properties in the one day as possible.

Unfortunately many investors (even those with a few properties) are so keen to buy property that they don't view enough to fully appreciate what they are buying. They think it will be okay and in most instances it usually does work out, but only because property is a pretty forgiving investment. I also often hear of horror stories from investors where it hasn't worked out.

Buying sight unseen can lead to many problems for the unsuspecting investor. I remember when I was looking for opportunities and came across a town with high yielding properties. At the time I didn't think much of it yet it caught Ed's attention and he decided to pursue it. The result was that we purchased a little three-bedroom property that was about 25 years old. The photos we received from the real estate agent showed the property to be in fairly good condition.

It wasn't until we saw the property some months later that I received the greatest shock. The property was in worse condition than I had anticipated. The backyard had become home to a stockpile of beer cans and mechanical spare parts. The tenant obviously had not maintained the property and it was not in the good condition I had seen in the photos that had been sent to me by the real estate agent. Had I seen the property before buying, we may not have bought it. In this instance buying sight unseen worked in our favour because of the high capital growth the area was experiencing at the time.

Solution
Buying sight unseen can work but you need to put certain processes in place to ensure there are no nasty surprises. As for our little property, we have now decided to bulldoze it and build three units on it which will provide us with a wonderful return. I am grateful there was the opportunity to do that otherwise, well who knows, it could have become the white elephant of our portfolio.

I learnt a lot from this experience and have especially learnt how to do it right next time round. I have now created a buying strategy and process that I go through religiously when buying sight unseen.

Here's my tip: there are five different people who need to view your property before you buy:

1) **Sales agent:** the sales agent needs to have viewed and valued the property for sale and know what it looks like, what the best features are and what the concerns are. We start off by obtaining as many photos from the sales agent as possible, especially the kitchen and bathrooms. These rooms are the most expensive to repair/replace so best to obtain photos that are close up and clear so you can see any repairs required. Photos of walls and doors give you an indication of whether they need to be repaired and/or repainted. You should also get photos of the streetscape and what the property next door is like. I had a client who looked at buying a little house which had appeal in the photos, however the building next door was an industrial laundromat with trucks coming and going all day. The photos saved my client from a potential disaster.

2) **Building inspector:** a building inspector should be employed to assess and identify any building issues. They too will usually take photos and highlight any concerns with the property. Building inspections are great in that they are usually thorough and give a clear indication of the structural and aesthetic condition of the property. This should be done prior to settlement and a satisfactory report should be a pre-condition to purchasing the property.

3) **Pest inspector:** a pest inspector assesses the property to ensure there are no creepy crawlies present that could cause potential damage to the building. The pest inspector's report also contains photos and gives an overview of the general condition of the property. This should be done prior to settlement and a satisfactory report should be a pre-condition to purchasing the property.

4) **Property manager's inspection:** the property manager's inspection is to check whether the property is in a liveable condition for a tenant to occupy. The best person to give you impartial advice on the condition of the property is the property manager. To ensure the property manager is not impacted by the selling agent, we usually get a property manager from another real estate agency to review the property. In that way there is no conflict of interest. The property manager is fantastic for assessing how rentable the property is, as well as the general condition of it. The last thing a property manager wants is a property that has been neglected and requires continuous attention. Properties like that are usually a great deal of work for property managers and hence when inspecting our potential property purchases, they give us a great indication of its condition. They also provide us with a number of photos and a general inspection report. A property manager can become your eyes and ears when purchasing sight unseen. This should be done prior to settlement and a satisfactory report should be a pre-condition to purchasing the property.

5) **Bank valuer inspection**: the bank valuer who is commissioned by the lender will assess the property for its value and provide a valuation which confirms that you have paid fair market value for that property. The fact that he/she has entered the property demonstrates the property exists and its value is accurate. The lender will insist this is done prior to settlement.

To ensure your investment purchase is a real living asset (pardon the pun), it's important that the above steps are undertaken prior to settling the purchase of the property. In this way, if I purchase sight unseen and have five different people go through the property, it must exist and there is a good chance that the condition of the property is reasonable and I won't have to spend squillions of dollars fixing it up.

It would be very difficult for five independent people to fudge the results. Making a decision to purchase a property sight unseen is a lot easier if you have all the photos, reports, feedback and assessments. If you ask enough questions, buying sight unseen can be a very successful and easy way to buy property without having to leave the comfort of your home.

Here's my other tip: don't stop asking questions. Talk to other locals, council members, local businesses etc. and obtain their feedback on the area or street you are buying in. Contact the pastor at the local church who has probably lived there most of his life – you'll be amazed how much he knows about the area. Or try contacting the senior citizens club and ask to speak to the longest standing member. They too are a wealth of information about what has gone on over the years. Often they will be more than happy to fill you in on all the local history – all 50 years of it!

One more thing; make sure you get comfortable when having this conversation as you could be there for a while.

Mistake 29 – Believing everything you hear

I am guilty of making this mistake and I couldn't believe it when it happened. I took shortcuts, thinking I was such an expert and didn't need to undertake all the necessary 'due diligence' research that was required to purchase a property.

Boy was I wrong and didn't it come home to roost!

It was our eighth property purchase and I was looking for a positive cash flow deal, which can be hard to find. I eventually found a property on the internet and proceeded to ring the real estate agent to ask more questions. The house was on the market for $179,000 and it had 12 months left on a five-year lease with options to extend it for another three years. The weekly rent was $330 – not bad for a little three-bedroom, one-bathroom, double-carport house. The house was in a sought after location and opposite a beautiful park. It was about 20 years old and in very good condition. At the time of buying the property, the market was hot and property prices were on the increase so negotiating a huge discount was difficult.

Anyway, I did my research, negotiated the price down to $173,000 and proceeded with the sale. The sales agent I was dealing with knew very little about the rental market in the area (you'd think this would have been a warning sign), however I proceeded to ask him what the property would rent for on the open market should the lease options not be extended. He told me it would rent 'easily' for $330 per week, if not more. Thinking I had hit the jackpot, I believed him and finalised the deal. We enjoyed the next 12 months of good cash flow. Unfortunately towards the end of the lease, we were notified that the lease would not be renewed. I wasn't too concerned at that point and immediately proceeded to arrange for the property manager to review the property and advertise for a new tenant.

The property manager reported that the property was in very good condition, the rental market was buoyant, that rentals were going up and that it would be easy to replace the tenant within a week or two. To my absolute horror, she quoted a rent of $260 per week. I was in shock. I explained to her what the sales agent had told me about the rent when I first purchased the property and she explained that because it was a company lease over a number of years, the rents usually ended up being above market value because they were automatically indexed to the inflation rate and not the market value of rent. Had I known this piece of information, I would clearly not have purchased this property. By believing what the sales agent had told me, the investment went from being positive cash flow to negative cash flow (according to the numbers) in one swoop.

Solution
Listen to sales agents but don't believe everything they tell you. Always cross-reference and/or validate what they have to say with other agents or experts. For the cost of a phone call I could have saved myself a lot of trouble. Instead, what I learnt in the process was priceless and, as a result, you can now benefit from my mistake. When dealing with sales agents a way of validating what they tell you is to ask the appropriate person. For example, the sales agent in question acknowledged that he did not know

anything about the rental market. I should therefore have questioned an independent property manager rather than listen to him.

For more thorough due diligence research, apart from speaking to an independent property manager, I should have cross-referenced what they told me with a second independent property manager from another company. This cross-referencing allows you as an investor to obtain a very good understanding of the rental market in the area you are looking to purchase property. Using a property manager from another company means you have someone who is independent of your property purchase. The more you cross reference your due diligence research with several property managers, the more reliable your information becomes.

We ended up selling this property 18 months later and due to the rising market, we made a small profit. My lesson here is to NEVER cut corners when undertaking my due diligence research. These days I am more thorough than when I started. I am not complacent about the research, nor do I take for granted that I know what I am doing. In this instance, I managed to learn the lesson without any financial loss, so please make sure you do your homework thoroughly before making your investment purchase.

In another example, I was once researching an area that was unfamiliar to me and when speaking to a sales agent, he told me a motorway was being built and that prices would go up in the area as a result. What I did to validate his information was to go to the website of the local council and search for this project. On the council website I was able to see that there were a number of projects that had already commenced or were scheduled to commence in that year. It was obvious the council was investing large amounts of money to improve infrastructure. From reading the website I could also ascertain that the council was 'family orientated' and was looking to attract families to the area. You are probably thinking 'so what' or 'what does that mean'? Well, if a council is actively trying to draw people (in particular families) to an area, as an investor, it gives me an idea of the type of accommodation people will want to live in. For example, a family consisting of a single mum with three children and a cat will not select a one-bedroom unit to live in. A three or four-bedroom house or unit would be more appropriate. So if the majority of people moving to/living in the area are families, then I would purchase a property that met my tenant's needs.

To get back to my point earlier about what sales agents tell us, listening to the sales agent meant I was then able to go more deeply into my investigations and discover what council was planning for the area. This in turn led to my discovery of the type of people moving into the area and it therefore narrowed down my search for the type of property I wanted to buy as a result.

Mistake 30 – Not knowing when to walk away

There are many investors who are so keen to get into the property market that they sometimes lose sight of whether the deal really works for them or not. They are so desperate to buy something that they become emotionally attached to the outcome and are unable to walk away from a transaction at a time when they really need to. Property investing is all about 'the numbers' and nothing else but the numbers.

An example of when investors fail to walk away from deals when they should is when negotiations between investor and vendor break down and agreement can't be reached. I've seen highly emotional investors hang in, offering more and more in the hope that the vendor will change his/her mind. While the investor is desperately trying to close the deal the vendor has the upper hand in the negotiation process and will push the investor to their maximum. If the vendor asks more than the investor was prepared to offer at the beginning of negotiations, then the investor should walk away from the deal and not come back until the vendor calls and accepts the investor's offer. The reasoning behind this is that as soon as the investor has walked away, the tables turn and the investor has the upper hand in the negotiations because the investor has signaled to the vendor that he/she is prepared to walk away and that if the vendor really wants the deal then he/she will have to call the investor back. If this occurs, the investor will know that the vendor has no other buyers and is desperate to sell. It is then that the investor should counter offer the vendor less again than he/she was prepared to offer in the first place and then negotiate around that price.

For example, I know of an investor who researched a particular area that she wanted to invest in. The area at the time was experiencing a boom in property prices and it became difficult to negotiate discounts. Each time a property came onto the market she would put in an offer well below the advertised price in the hope the vendor would accept. To make the numbers work, her purchase price for her intended deal needed to be low and she spent hours negotiating a price on all the properties that came onto the market in the area. It was obvious these deals would not work, as many of the properties were achieving values well above the vendor's asking price. She continued to put in offers, but to no avail. In the end she was emotionally drained, disheartened, ended up with nothing and wasted precious time on an area that just wasn't going to work for her.

Solution
I admire any investor who has enough determination and gumption to work hard at securing a great deal. There comes a point in time, however, when it's best to walk away and invest your precious time and energy in researching other areas that better fit your yield and growth requirements. Use the numbers to dictate whether you pursue a deal or not. The numbers will help you to keep the emotion out of the deal. It is important that you understand that and know when to walk away.

Further to the previous example, this investor discussed the matter with me at length and I was able to ascertain that her level of knowledge was very detailed in relation to the area. With some mentoring from me, she expanded her search to other areas that had a similar profile and almost instantly was able to secure a fantastic property. The numbers worked, the due diligence research also stacked up, all the key criteria were met and she was able to successfully close the deal.

Here's my tip: be prepared to walk away as the next best deal comes around at least once a week.

Mistake 31 – Hey big spender

Unless you are in the trade or are an expert in calculating building costs, most amateur house renovators I speak to overcapitalise on their renovations. By this I mean that the cost of the house with renovations exceeds the market price for similar houses in that particular area. My personal experience has been that in most instances it is easier and cheaper to rip down an existing house and construct a new one than to renovate the existing one. There are investors who enjoy getting their hands dirty and creating something new. Television shows have made renovating fashionable and people (without any real knowledge) have got caught up in the hype of wanting to personally renovate their own home or their investment properties. The mistake here is that many people underestimate the time and money required to complete the job.

Not everyone overcapitalises on renovations, however it is really easy to overspend on them. Investors who have done it right have obtained many quotes before starting and kept within their budget. I had a friend who recently obtained quotes for a fence she wanted built on her property. She went to many fencing companies seeking a quote for a particular type of fence. As she knew exactly what she wanted, all companies received the same information and to her surprise, the quotes varied from $2000 to $4000.

She had a budget of $1000 to build this fence and the above demonstrates how easy it is to get it wrong and end up doubling (or more) your costs for the renovation.

Solution
If you are an amateur and want to renovate, as a guide, work out your costs and then double them. Estimate the amount of time needed to do the renovation and then triple it. This will generally be a more accurate picture of what really happens. Is it any wonder that marital relationships suffer during renovation. And

it is worse still if you are living in the house while you are renovating it.

My husband and I have been renovating our 1925 Californian Bungalow for the past five years. We almost separated over the choice of colour for the walls. We painted our guest room five times and just could not agree on a colour. We ended up hiring a colour consultant who worked with the style of the house and with the colours that we had already selected. Within five minutes of her arrival she opened up her colour chart and our frustrations had come to an end. The solution to our colour selection was solved – Regency White!

Hiring a colour consultant was a great investment as not only did she save our marriage, she saved us money. We had purchased so many paint pots that we could literally have opened up our own paint shop. Use the experts – that's what they are there for and it's their specialty. We all like to think we are decorators and handy with tools, however consider the real cost of doing it all yourself compared to bringing in the experts.

Part 4 – Property Management

Mistake 32 – DIY property management

I usually recommend to my clients that they manage their first investment property by themselves. It gives them a good insight into how much property managers actually do to earn the relatively small management fee they receive each week. We managed our first property ourselves and I will never repeat the experience. Our first tenant was a single woman who lived on her own. The property was a double-storey townhouse and was local to where we lived so she knew we were not far away should something need doing.

She kept the house in immaculate condition so no complaints there. However twice she locked the garage door with the key and then used the remote control to try to open it. Twice I needed to get it repaired and in a hurry. The ducted heating caused the upstairs area to get very hot while the downstairs area was cold (heat rises). We purchased and arranged installation for another heater downstairs in the lounge room to make it more comfortable for her. She wanted to convert one of the bedrooms into a study so I arranged for the telephone company to come out and install new points.

She then wanted security doors so she would feel safe. No problem, I bought the best security doors on the market as a woman alone should feel safe. When there was a serious storm that caused water to leak into the roof space and on the ceiling, we received the call at night. The new dishwasher somehow managed to shake a bit when turned on, we needed to fix that too. The clothes line needed tensioning, we repaired that. Lawns needed mowing, we attended to that. She wanted to hang pictures on the walls and wanted our approval, we approved that. The baton lights were not good enough, so we bought light fittings. Plus the front door bell stopped working, so we fixed that (she had put a new battery in the wrong way). We also purchased hoses for her to water the garden, one for the front and one for the back which she did not use.

She is a lovely lady and these days (she has moved on) we stay in touch and enjoy her company. We spent many weekends fixing, repairing, mowing and listening just to save $25 a week in management fees. We could have spent that time more profitably researching other areas to invest in.

Solution

After my own personal experience I can honestly say that property managers earn every cent they make. I have learnt my lesson and will never manage a property again. My time is worth more than $25 so why would I spend the time managing my investment properties? Look at how you can best spend your time instead of running after tenants. Let your property managers receive the calls at all hours, let them follow up when the rent is not paid, let them arrange for tradespeople to fix things when they break down.

Think about it this way, let's assume your property management fees are 10 per cent. Your average one year old rental property is earning you, say, $240 per week in rent. Therefore your property manager would earn $24 per week for managing your property. What happens if the dishwasher stops working or is not working effectively? The tenant is complaining that the dishwasher leaks and is keen to get it fixed as they are too busy to wash dishes by hand. Your property manager quickly contacts you to explain the problem. You suggest that as the property is only a year old, the dishwasher should be under warranty. You also explain that the user guide for the dishwasher was left in the kitchen drawer with all the other instruction booklets when the tenant moved in. The property manager now contacts the tenant, trying to locate the user guide in order to find out the model number of the dishwasher to contact the company in relation to the warranty. The tenant says they will call back with the details when they get home from work. The tenant fails to call back and the property manager gets busy with other matters. Several days later, the property manager is playing telephone tag with the tenant and rings you to advise they have yet to obtain the details. A week goes by and the dishwasher is still not repaired.

Eventually the property manager gets hold of the tenant who can't find the booklet. It takes another week of to-ing and fro-ing before the booklet is found and the model number obtained. The property manager rings the manufacturer to discover that the dishwasher is now one month out of warranty. You are then contacted by the property manager and told that your tenant is extremely unhappy. You then advise them to obtain three quotes for the repair. The property manager does so and faxes you the quotes seeking further instruction. You select your preferred quote and the property manager organises the repair and inspects the work that has been carried out correctly… blah, blah, blah.

The property manager has made countless calls to you, the tenant and tradespeople. He/she would have personally gone out to the property (as I would have requested that they sight the completed repairs and provide evidence of it) and also faxed you the quotes for approval. They would have spent many hours dealing with this issue and all for $24 per week. It is the cheapest labour you will ever find and if your property happens to be older and in need of more maintenance, then your property manager will most definitely earn his/her fee.

Here's my tip: look at property management fees as a cost of doing business and a small cost at that. It saves you the headache of attending to maintenance issues or if a tenant does not pay the rent. Rather than resent the fees, appreciate the work that property managers do when things need attention. You may not realise it but your property manager assists you in your wealth creation plan.

Mistake 33 – Keeping it in the family

You might think renting your investment property to family would be a great idea – WRONG! Unless you have the perfect functional family that never argues, supports each other unconditionally and is always there to help out when needed, never rent your property out to family. If you do have the perfect family, if it does really exist, please send me an email and tell me all about them. I would be interested in talking to someone who has experienced 'perfection'. For the rest of us who come from, shall we say 'interesting' families, sharing your asset with family members can become your biggest nightmare. I have a friend who realised his superannuation fund would not sustain him in retirement so he decided to purchase an investment property as part of his nest egg. Being the great dad that he is, he decided to rent his investment property to his young adult son at a much-reduced rate. My friend worked hard to pay the mortgage each month. His son didn't appreciate his father's generosity and did not look after the place. His son also didn't pay the rent when it was due. In addition to this, his son moved his new girlfriend in who also did not make any contribution to the rent. The result for my friend was that his new 'retirement plan' was fast becoming a charity for his son and girlfriend.

The financial pressure started to impact on my friend so he decided to sell the property in order to clear the debt and get his son and his girlfriend out of the property. Things turned nasty when he asked his son to move out. The 'clever son' deliberately left the house in a mess so when prospective buyers went through the house they walked out disgusted at the poor condition that the property was kept in. We've seen it on television – family members crying that a relative is throwing them out on the street and how horrid they are. What the news story fails to say is that the family member has not paid rent for many months and expected to live in the property for free.

There can sometimes be an expectation by family members that as you have the investment property, you are rich enough and can afford to have them living there for free. What family may not understand is that the rent is needed to pay for the mortgage and the expenses to own the property.

Solution
If you really enjoy the pain of renting your property to family then consider employing a property manager to manage the property. Have the property manager collect the rent, obtain the bond and conduct regular inspections. In this way you can have the property manager take care of the official business of looking after your investment property while you enjoy the relationship with your family.

Here's my tip: if things go wrong with the property, direct the family member to report it to the property manager as they will take care of it, once again separating business from family. It's also important to have landlord's insurance and all the normal processes as if you were renting the property to a stranger.

It is true when they say that "business and family do not mix". It's like trying to mix water with oil.

Mistake 34 – Selecting your property manager

Have you noticed that most property managers are really young, inexperienced and have a lot to learn? Too many investors fail to interview their property manager to find out whether they have the necessary skills, knowledge, experience, capacity and resources to successfully manage your property. If a property manager has 400 properties to look after, how much time do you think they will have to spend dealing with your property issues? If a property manager has just moved into the area, how will he/she know what tenants in that area want? If a property manager is not proactive, how many problems do you think you might have?

Have you heard of the tenants from hell or of a property so badly maintained that no one will rent it? Property managers can be your best friend or your worst nightmare. If they are proactive and do their job efficiently and effectively, the result is usually a very good investment for you, the investor.

Solution

Interview your property managers before engaging them to manage your property. We only engage property managers who have met strict assessment criteria, including making sure that any one person who manages property in the agency:

- only looks after up to a maximum of 200 properties,
- has a very good understanding of what tenants in the area want,
- knows the area well and is proactive in dealing with tenants (anything less is unacceptable),
- has had at least five years managing properties, and
- has to be qualified and trained to manage properties.

Property management agencies should have computerised property management systems that allow for automatic and direct debit and payment facilities and issue resolution tracking. They should also have the capability to pay all expenses on your behalf, including insurances, body corporate fees and rates.

As a rule, I authorise my property managers to spend up to $300 without having to consult me first for any maintenance issues that need attention. For example, if the taps need the washers changed, then I am happy for my property managers to organise the plumber and get it fixed.

However, one thing I make abundantly clear to all my property managers is that if I find out the tenant has been complaining about something and it was not rectified in a timely manner and I was not told about it, then they are fired. They get no second chances. We treat our tenants like gold. We look after our tenants because they look after our investment, which in turn is growing us wealth. Rather than treat our tenants with disdain (as so many investors do), we prefer to treat them as our greatest asset.

For example, one of our properties had water leaking through the roof due to bad weather and heavy rain. The water was leaking through a cracked roof tile onto the ceiling in the bedroom, which would have caused water damage to the plaster. It could have resulted in electrical problems plus the need for the ceiling to be repainted due to the water damage. Instead the tenant got into the roof and placed a bucket under the drip to prevent any water damage. My property manager immediately organised repair of the roof and I organised a bottle of wine for my tenants to thank them for their efforts. Had they not addressed the problem when they did, the repair costs would have been significantly higher. Showing appreciation to my tenant – priceless!

So make sure you interview your property managers and find one that will look after you and your tenant.

Mistake 35 – No landlords insurance

How many investors don't have landlords insurance? Research shows about 60 per cent of investors have no idea what it is. Landlords insurance is one of the cheapest forms of insurance you can purchase and is a must if you are a property investor who wants to sleep comfortably at night. Most sensible people I know wouldn't drive a car without some form of insurance so why would you invest hundreds of thousands of dollars in property and not have it properly insured?

Landlords insurance gives you peace of mind knowing that whatever happens you are covered. Landlord's insurance covers things that are not included in building and contents insurance and is specifically for investment properties, as the name suggests. More specifically a good landlord's insurance policy covers things like:

- Repair of malicious and accidental damage by the tenant and loss of rent during repair of the damage,
- Theft by tenant,
- Loss of rent,
- Legal liability,
- Rent default if a tenant absconds without paying the rent,
- Rent default during the period it takes to evict a tenant,
- Rent default if the tenant stays and does not pay rent,
- Legal and court costs.

Check your policies in detail, as there are good policies and not so good policies. Especially make sure that you are covered for rent default. This covers rental loss for the period when the tenant has not paid you rent and you need to go to court to obtain the money and/or evict the tenant from your property. Good landlord's insurance policies will also cover legal and court costs.

We regularly see on news segments landlords who cry foul because their tenants have been difficult to deal with. On many occasions the right insurance would have covered the issue.

A friend of mine leased her property to a family with young children. They were the perfect tenants. The husband had a solid and stable job, earning enough to sustain his family. His wife stayed home looking after their youngest child while the older children attended the local school. The wife maintained the home beautifully as if it were her own. Sounds rosy doesn't it?

No one banked on this lovely couple separating. The husband left his wife and children. As she didn't work, she relied on him to continue paying the rent. However he needed to rent elsewhere and required the cash to cover his costs, which stretched their finances while they battled out their personal circumstances.

Unfortunately my friend, the landlord, was caught up in the crossfire and needed to go to court to evict them and claim their bond in order to cover their arrears.

Thankfully, she had landlords insurance. Had this not been the case, she would have been thousands of dollars out of pocket. Why go through the pain and expense of trying to take a tenant to court when the insurance policy can cover all of these items, including the rental arrears?

Solution
There are at least three types of insurance you will need to have to protect your investment. These are:
- building insurance
- contents insurance
- landlord's insurance

Some insurance companies package all three into one package and call it landlords insurance, but others only offer individual policies for each.

Check your insurance policies carefully to see that all areas are covered

Your property manager will know all about landlords insurance and can recommend reputable companies that provide you with copies of their policies if you require assistance. Alternatively, your property managers will, as part of their fee, organise to take the insurance out for you but if you do get them to take it out, make sure they have completely covered your property for everything you require to be covered. Landlords insurance becomes part of your exit strategy, your back-up plan for if things go wrong. If you have done all the checks on your tenant and on paper they are perfect, it may not take much for them to become your biggest nightmare. People's lives change, which can impact on their ability to pay the rent. As the rent from the tenant generally covers the mortgage payments on the property, it is really important to have insurance so you are not left out of pocket should something go wrong.

Here's my tip: if you are going to be a property investor, then I suggest you invest in all three insurances and especially landlords insurance. Consider it a cost of doing business. If you pay peanuts for the policy, you will get monkeys, so be careful, double check your excesses and make sure you read all the inclusions and fine print and don't be afraid to shop around.

Mistake 36 – Treating the tenant badly

I am always surprised by landlords who treat their tenants badly. Let's look at this for a moment. A good tenant generally pays the rent on time, looks after the gardens, keeps the property in good condition, doesn't have regular wild parties or hold the weekly Hell's Angels get-togethers so why treat them badly?

Landlords wonder why tenants do not stay, break leases and move on. Having been a tenant myself I understand how an uncooperative landlord encourages tenants to move out. For example, when I was renting a two-year-old, two-bedroom townhouse about six years ago, I really looked after the place and made it my home. I met my legal obligations of keeping the gardens well maintained and everything was kept in excellent working order. I regularly steam cleaned the carpets and generally lived a quiet life. The unit was on a corner block with walls facing north and west. In winter it was okay but in summer it was a hot box. I sweltered through two summers in that hot box and vowed I wouldn't live through another summer in it unless air conditioning was installed. Even on a cooler day in summer, the unit would quickly warm up. I spoke to the property manager and requested that the landlord install an air conditioner in at least one bedroom, which was upstairs. I even offered to pay more rent if the landlord put in the air conditioning.

It took months before the landlord responded that he might install one but it depended on the cost. Finally, after much haggling, he offered a little one horse powered unit to be placed into the sliding glass doors in the master bedroom. The master bedroom only had sliding glass doors leading out onto a very small balcony, so placing the air conditioning unit in the door would mean that the remainder of the sliding door would have had to be boarded up and I would never have been able to open the door again. The sliding door was my only source of fresh air into the bedroom. The landlord could have mounted the single horse powered unit onto the wall however he didn't want to do that.

I got so sick and tired of haggling that I moved out. The landlord lost a perfectly good tenant by making the pain of staying greater than the pain of leaving, and all for a few hundred dollars. He lost more money in having the property vacant for a couple of weeks while he found a new tenant and on passing by the property months later, it was obvious that the new tenants were not looking after the property the way I did. The property went from looking like an owner-occupied property to a rundown rental.

Solution
Many investors do not consider the cost of finding a new tenant. I am not saying that you spend all your money on keeping the tenant pleased, however being prepared to look after the tenants will pay dividends in the end, as tenants will generally reciprocate and look after the property.

For example, a friend of mine has several investment properties and each year at Christmas time she always organises for the property manager to deliver a Christmas card and gift basket to her tenants, thanking them for looking after the property. She has also been known to offer the tenants a slab or two of the golden ale if that is their preference. I also do the same thing for my tenants and have offered movie tickets and/or gift vouchers, depending on where the properties are located and what the tenants prefer. As mentioned in a previous mistake, the tenant went above and beyond by attending to the broken roof tile and in so doing prevented extensive damage being done to my property, hence a bottle of wine is a relatively inexpensive thank you.

In my experience, here are the key standard things tenants ask for:

Fly screens – to keep the flies out.
Security doors – so they can leave the front door open for fresh air.
Garden shed – for storing their garden equipment and tools.
Remotes – on garage doors, especially if they are double doors.
Foxtel – as long as they pay for the installation and connection.
Air conditioning – if the property continually gets hot.
Plants – they are often happy to plant them in the garden themselves as long as I reimburse their costs.
Painting – again tenants are happy to paint the room if I cover the cost of the paint.

In reality tenants are reasonable people trying to create a home in which to live, just like you and I. By treating them well, you will effectively ensure that your investment is protected. Be kind to them and if they want you to repair something – fix it and don't complain.

Mistake 37 – Not increasing the rent

There are so many investors who literally give their money away by not increasing the rent on their properties annually. They struggle from week to week to sustain their investment property yet give their money away to their tenants by providing them with under priced accommodation. I hear it all the time from investors... "they are good tenants so I didn't put the rent up because I don't want to lose them". Some of these tenants have been in these properties for years with no rental increases, yet property costs such as council and water rates, insurances and mortgage interest rates have all risen and the investor/landlord is taking the hit each time. I can understand not putting up the rent for a couple of years, but anything beyond that is just plain ridiculous. For example, I met an investor recently who had a property he was renting to a single parent with one child. He was renting it for $160 per week and had done so for four years without any rental increases. At that time, the market value of rent in the area for his property was $280 per week – a difference of $120 per week. If you look at that figure over a year, it was a loss of $6240 per year. Over the four years he had missed out on a whopping $24,960 in income. What could you do with an extra $25,000? His argument for giving the tenant a lower rent was that the tenant was a single parent who looked after the place. Property investing is a business and you need to treat it as such.

This example illustrates that the investor was giving away a large amount of money by not increasing the rent because a) he had a good tenant and b) the tenant was a single parent. These are emotional decisions which have no room in the business of property investing if you want to survive in it. If you go broke and have to sell your investment properties because you have been overly kind to tenants, then you have effectively taken rental properties off the market. This means someone is now deprived of a potential home to live in and all because you didn't run your business properly. Another way of looking at it is that property investors are in fact providing community housing that the government is not providing. For an investor to be able to able to continue to provide community accommodation rents must be increased to cover increasing costs.

Solution

From my experience, if you increase the rent and keep it just below or at market value for rent in the area of your investment property then the tenant will not move. They might move for other reasons but it won't be because you put up the rent. The tenant will realise that if they move it will be to another place where the rent will most likely be about the same. They will therefore accept the increase and pay it. They will come to the conclusion that the cost and hassle of moving to another place just won't be worth it. I don't want to sound like a broken record however as already mentioned in previous chapters, property investing is a business and businesses are run on numbers. To maximise the numbers in your property investing business so that you grow your wealth, you will need to increase your rental returns regularly.

To know when to increase your rents and by how much, you should consult with your property manager at least annually. You will need to gauge whether it is appropriate to increase the rent at that particular time, taking into consideration such things as:
- What the current market value of rent is for your investment property,
- What the likely impact is if the market has increased,
- How many vacant investment properties like yours there are in the area,
- What the capacity is for your tenant to pay the increase.

An increase of $5 or $10 will not break the bank for your tenant, as the cost of moving out will be more expensive than paying the small increase. Where the problem lies is when a tenant has not had a rental increase for many years and you then decide you want to put it up by a lot in order to bring it to market value. They are well within their rights to object to such a huge increase.

Here's my tip: increase rents in small regular amounts that will allow you to cover your increases in costs. This in turn will allow the tenant to get used to paying small increases and allow him/her to manage the increases progressively.

Part 5 – What Are You Thinking?

Mistake 38 – In one ear and out the other

The most expensive advice you can get is from a poor person and unless your friends and family have achieved the level of financial success you want to achieve, you'd be wise to seek your advice elsewhere. Friends and family only want to protect you, but sometimes their own fears and insecurities can prevent you from creating wealth and financial security.

When I started to learn about property investing years ago, many of my friends, family and business colleagues all said I was crazy and that I would lose money. In fact when I told them I'd paid thousands of dollars to attend property seminars they thought I was on another planet. I remember feeling at one point that maybe I had made a mistake, that I'd spent my money on a property education program that would not work and would have to live with the embarrassment of it all. When I started I had no money, I borrowed the thousands of dollars from the bank to participate in the program and I was renting a little two-bedroom unit. We had no savings, no equity and no knowledge. We knew getting into property investing was the way to go but we didn't know how. So our logic told us to get an education which we spent thousands doing. All we had going for us were our day jobs; we were paid relatively well.

How quickly my family and friends were to criticise me and gossip about what I was trying to achieve. I understood they were concerned for me however it still didn't make it easy. It's amazing how the negative thoughts started to creep into my mind and I started to doubt myself. I went through that while being laughed at by those around me. I decided to no longer talk to anyone about what I was doing unless they were an investor themselves and understood what I was trying to achieve.

It took a while but I eventually got there. I found more and more people like me trying to create wealth through property investing. It was fabulous talking to like-minded people about strategies and techniques as well as sharing contacts within my networks. I found the education program exhilarating and, as a result, went on to build a multi-million dollar property portfolio with no equity and no savings – only the income that Ed and I received from our jobs. Today we have continued to educate ourselves through reading books, attending seminars and by having personal mentors.

As for our family and friends, well we had a national magazine write an article about us and our rags to riches story. I had the greatest pleasure in buying lots of copies of the magazine and distributing it to our friends and family to read. The look on their faces when they read about our financial achievements... priceless! If I had listened to them, I wouldn't be enjoying a lifestyle that has come from property investing. Instead, I would be slaving away in the rat race hanging out for the weekend to come. A day job will not make you rich and listening to people who prevent you from creating wealth can cost you dearly.

Solution
Get involved with groups or clubs of like-minded investors where you can continue to grow and learn without ridicule, somewhere where you can seek out support and encouragement. You will be amazed at how many like-minded people there are out there. Try not to openly talk about wealth creation with

friends and family until you have produced results. This will make your life easier.

Many people suffer from the tall poppy syndrome in Australia and most rich people I know deliberately keep a low profile and stay under the radar with what they have created. However, if you are to ask them about what they have done to achieve wealth and success, you may get a wonderful surprise. They are usually more than happy to share their techniques and secrets.

I had a client who recently told me her family was against her joining our mentoring program. The family was also upset when my client purchased a house off the plan. It's amazing how, now that the house is being built, her family is proud and encouraging others in the family to do the same. It often takes proof to convince people you know about the merit of what you are doing and that purchasing investment properties is the way to go.

Here's my tip: I once went to a seminar where I listened to a property multi-millionaire speak about his strategies for investing. One thing he said that will always remain with me was, "when you have made it in the game of investing, always go back to that one negative person who tried to bring you down so that you can prove them wrong". I am not advocating vengeful behaviour, however it does feel damn good!

Mistake 39 – Being a know-it-all

As I spend many of my waking hours mentoring clients and teaching them how to build a successful property portfolio, I always come across one or two people who think they know everything. These are the people who constantly say "I know..."

My latest passion is understanding human behaviour and one of the many discoveries I have made is that people who constantly say "I know..." in a conversation are not actually listening, and in their failure to listen they never really get to know. In a similar manner, people who repeatedly say "to be honest with you..." in a conversation are actually being dishonest.

When I meet people who think they know everything when really they clearly do not, it makes me laugh. Their ego gets in the way. I'm not sure if it is because I am female (young and gorgeous – okay, just kidding) or whether they feel they need to prove themselves.

Anyway, when I start sharing with such people some of my strategies on how to successfully invest in property, the response I get from them is that they already know everything that I am talking about. At this point, I am really happy they know so much as I love talking to educated investors. So I proceed to ask them how many properties they have, thinking they have amassed a multi-million dollar portfolio and I am keen to compare notes. It never fails to surprise me (and you would think that I would learn to pick it) when they tell me they have not purchased any property and go into giving me all the reasons why they haven't – or should I say excuses. One such person explained to me that he had been watching the property market for 10 years and rattled off all the names of courses and seminars he had been to. This guy has done them all – I guess you would call him a 'seminar junkie'. However although he knew the theory, he took no action and therefore had not produced any results – in 10 years!

For some reason about 90 per cent of people who attend wealth creation seminars never end up putting into action what they have learned.

Solution
There is a wealth of knowledge out there if you are only willing to open your mind and listen. Like every other type of investing, property can be a mug's game if you don't know how to do it. It is, however, more forgiving than most other asset classes. I have come to realise that even those we distrust have something to offer. Leaving the ego at home and learning to listen might just result in you becoming wealthier in all aspects of your life.

Here's my tip: be prepared to listen. Even if you think you know, you might just be surprised at just how little you really do know. Be wary of anyone who has a vested interest in the outcome giving you advice (i.e. a financial gain such as a sales commission). Salespeople generally live off their commissions and some might stretch the truth in order to gain a sale. If in doubt as to whether a commission is at the end of the advice being given to you, ask.

I am not saying ignore advice. All I am saying is that you should validate the information being given to you if there is a commission involved. Sales agents can be a wealth of information but just be wary of accepting the advice as if it were a trusted source.

Old Chinese proverb: "Arrogance is the problem of the fool".

Mistake 40 – Don't be a wannabe forever

Tell me if you can relate to this: you are someone who is motivated enough to write down your goals. So you sit down and think of all the sorts of things you would like to do and have. You may even go so far as to categorise your goals in health, money, travel, relationships etc. and you may then even discuss your goals with your partner and/or friends. Once complete, you feel good about yourself for having committed them to paper. You then file away your goals in a bookcase or another safe place. Some months, or even years later, you rediscover your goals while doing a major clean-up of the room. You are looking down at your goals wondering why it was you never achieved any of them. Like, hello! I have seen magic before but this is ridiculous. How do you expect to achieve your goals by having them locked away in some bookcase?

Get your list of goals out of the bookcase, enlarge them so you can read them from three metres away and then splash copies of them across every available wall space in your house, including the toilet wall, so that you can't miss seeing them at least three times a day. In that way they become firmly implanted in your power house (your subconscious) and once they are there, they are there for life or until you change them. Either way your subconscious won't let you rest until you've achieved them.

The point here is that your subconscious will put your goals on the backburner as quick as lightning if you hide them in a bookcase. You need to live, breathe and reinforce them in your subconscious constantly if you want to successfully turn your current 'rat race' mentality around. Believe me, it takes a bit of discipline but the result is fantastic.

Goals won't happen by themselves so you'll need to develop a detailed plan of how you are going to achieve your goals. You'll then have to self-commit to taking the necessary actions required to complete the plan. This means getting off the couch and doing more than complain about what someone else has that you don't have. They've got it because they set themselves goals, they have then planned how they were going to achieve them and then they took the necessary actions to get them.

Most successful investors will set and review their goals at least twice a year. If you want to invest successfully, then you will need to set yourself goals that are consistent with your investment strategy. You will only be able to successfully set and/or review your goals when you are in a creative mood. In order to get into a creative mood you will need to be in the right environment. That is to say you won't be able to set meaningful goals in the middle of a football game or in a house full of screaming kids. You will need to get away for a couple of days with your partner to a relaxed environment and allow your mind to just breathe and you'll find that your creative ability to set goals that are really meaningful to you will happen naturally.

It only takes 21 days to create a habit, so start today by creating the habit of becoming rich. You can start by thinking about and writing down what it is you really want out of life. To not set goals means you are going through life blindly and missing out on a whole lot of life's fantastic opportunities.

Solution
Review your goals regularly, scrapping those that didn't work and keeping or modifying those that did. The important thing is that the goals you set are consistent with your overall investment

strategy. After a while this process will become more and more meaningful and filled with direction.

Goal setting needs to be realistic. It is therefore important that you set goals with action plans. What this achieves is that it gets you focused on taking the action necessary to achieving your goals.

I personally use the SMART process for setting goals. This stands for Specific, Measurable, Action, Realistic and Timely. Here is an example of how to write a goal using this process.

I will purchase one investment property costing no more than $250,000 with a positive cash flow of $20 per week after tax. I will undertake three months of due diligence on the selected area(s) with the intention of purchasing by 30th June (insert year).

Specific – purchase one investment property
Measurable – positive cash flow of $20 per week after tax.
Three months of due diligence.
Action – conduct due diligence and purchase property.
Realistic – investment property to cost no more than $250,000.
Timely – 30th June (insert year)

Your goal may be to purchase an investment property that starts you on your path to create wealth, which the above goal is perfect for. In order to achieve your goal, you will need to take action. Your actions may include reading books, going to seminars and finding an experienced property investor to mentor you.

As you build your knowledge and guidance from people who have successfully achieved what it is you want (to buy investment properties), then your goal becomes easier and more achievable.

Here's my tip: if you are serious about setting goals and taking action, please email me at info@realwealthaustralia.com.au with 'goal setting template' in the subject title and I will gladly email you a template for setting goals and taking action.

In the words of Nike – "just do it".

Mistake 41 – It's all in the mind

Property investing is 90 per cent mindset and 10 per cent knowledge. Without the proper mindset you may as well stop going to all those property seminars you may have been going to because you are just wasting your time.

What I mean by this is that you need to have the right mindset to invest in property successfully. People with the right mindset are those with the ability to think abundantly and positively toward achieving their goals. Once you've adopted the right mindset then it can be applied successfully to all aspects of your life.

Mindset is the difference between being able to successfully create wealth and staying poor. Funnily enough most poor people are stopped from investing by their fear of becoming rich. That is, they don't know if they will be able to handle being wealthy so they think up all the reasons in the world why being rich is bad. Phrases like, 'money is the root of all evil', 'my friends won't like me if I'm different' and 'he probably stole it or is into drugs' typify the typical mindset of the poor. The poverty mindset usually results in people creating fears and limiting beliefs in their ability to do things outside their comfort zone. This stems from their insecurities and lack of general knowledge. A wealthy person's mindset, on the other hand, is one that is inspired by what someone else has created and achieved. The rich mindset continues to learn and develop from their mistakes, whereas the poor cringe and slink away, never to return when they make a mistake.

There are investors who mentally struggle with borrowing money. Their mindset around money is negative, as they do not understand the difference between good debt and bad debt. They think all debt is bad and should be avoided. Whereas experienced investors want to bring on the good debt.

Solution
Many of my clients initially have negative feelings towards borrowing large amounts of money. Once they understand the difference between good debt and bad debt it's amazing how their perspective changes. Understanding debt and how to make it work for you rather than against you opens up another world, a world of wealth creation.

I really enjoy it when my clients have a breakthrough and begin to implement their very own and personal wealth creation strategy. They have confidence, show direction and have an attitude and mindset of abundance.

Here's my tip: there are many books on the market that will help you with your mindset. I have included a list of recommended reading in part 6 of this book.

Mistake 42 – Stop talking, start doing

Procrastination usually comes from fear, usually a fear of failure. We have all procrastinated at some time or other in our lives, yet when it comes to property investing I see people procrastinate even more than normal. In most cases it's because they are about to spend hundreds of thousands of dollars on an investment property and they can't decide whether they are doing the right thing or whether they are about to make a huge financial mistake that will ruin them. Procrastination can totally stop people from taking any action at all.

As some of my clients read this I know they will be thinking I am writing about them. Well I am, but not in a sinister way. It's important to understand that procrastination will hit all of us at least once in our lifetime. The real challenge is in how we deal with it and move forward.

My clients have regularly come across some of the best property deals that could be found at that time and do nothing about them, except tell others how great a deal was. As their mentor, getting clients over their procrastination is my biggest challenge.

For example, one of my favourite clients who I have known for many years (well before he became my client) would research upcoming hotspots years before the area would boom. His research showed the areas had excellent rental returns and potential for great capital growth. As it turned out, the areas he researched did boom, housing prices doubled within three years in one area and rental yields skyrocketed to 14 per cent. How many properties did he buy? One!

He procrastinated and missed out on some serious wealth creation. Since becoming my client he has gone on to build a significant portfolio of investment properties but wishes he had not procrastinated as much.

Solution
There are many ways to deal with procrastination but I find there are three that will usually do the trick.
One way is to put off procrastinating for another day.

The second is to deal with the fear that is plaguing you into procrastination at the time. For example, if you feel your due diligence is inadequate and you are in fear of making a major financial mistake, seek expert advice to help you understand and mitigate your fear.

The third is to write down all the reasons that have stopped you at that moment. Let's assume you want to buy a great investment property that you have found. You have done your homework but your gut feeling is telling you to not proceed. Usually the gut feeling is negative so it's important to deal with it rather than ignore it. Start by writing down what you are unsure of. What else do you need to know? What piece of the puzzle are you missing? Asking yourself these questions causes you to deal with the negative gut feeling. You then need to try and find the information you are missing to satisfy or overcome your gut feeling. Doing this will alleviate your concerns and give you more peace of mind. No point sacrificing your peace of mind just for an investment property.

Here's my tip: the more we procrastinate, the more we miss out. Like my favourite client, had he not dealt with the concerns that caused him to procrastinate, he would not have gone on to build a fantastic property portfolio.

Mistake 43 – Chickening out

We all fear making a financial loss but when it comes to property investing the loss can be huge. Getting the right education allows you to make educated investment decisions based on fact and logic rather than emotion and will take the fear out of the investment decision.

Fear usually relates to a lack of knowledge and many first-time investors I have met over the years are reluctant to move forward through the unknown. Yet at the same time when I suggest they go to seminars or read some books, again they refuse or give me a lame excuse – a logic that is foreign to me.

I usually face my fears and overcome them so they do not plague me or stop me from moving forward. I understand we don't want to make mistakes, especially huge financial ones that impact our lifestyles and families, yet knowledge is power and learning from people who have invested successfully allows you to minimise any mistakes you may make.

There seems to be a thought among western societies that asking for help is a sign of weakness. People would rather feel the fear of financial failure or of not knowing and then trying to bumble their way through than seeking advice from experienced people who have done it before. Not asking for assistance is the cause of people making mistakes and these mistakes can be disastrous when property is involved. I can relate to this very well. While working in the corporate world for a high profile, blue chip company, the culture was that you did not ask for help. There was an expectation that you should know what needed to be done and be able to execute it without assistance. The funny part about this type of corporate culture was that many people I worked with spent more time pretending to know something in order to be seen as being 'in the know'. The irony was there were more productive hours being spent 'looking good' and 'being in the know' than actually getting any work done.

I have noticed that this type of thinking is commonplace with most people. I have even noticed it with some of my clients. When they first join our programs, they give the impression that they understand when in actual fact they really don't. For example, I had a client who purchased a great property and wanted to renovate it. Part of their strategy was to commence renovating prior to settlement of the property. The renovation took about four weeks to complete. During it, they advertised the property for rent however endeavoured to achieve a high rental return by asking for above market rent. This is okay to do if you have time on your side, but they allowed the property to sit there untenanted for weeks without reviewing their asking price for rent.

Out of frustration, they discussed the matter with me and instantly we discussed lowering the rent to market value in which they quickly obtained a tenant. The problem here was that the matter could have been solved sooner had they not been blocked by their fear. Thinking they knew what they were doing caused them to make a financial mistake. Fortunately for them, the renovation provided them with a huge increase in the value of the property which in turn allowed them to enjoy a high rate of return on their investment.

Solution

In the words of Brian Tracey, "the world belongs to the askers". To reduce your fears of making a financial mistake, it is really important that you speak to people such as your mentors regarding your concerns. I have no doubt they have experienced the same doubts and fears you have somewhere along the way.

If you want to take action and get into property investing now, then take the time to learn, learn and learn. The knowledge you gain through reading books such as this one, attending seminars and joining mentoring programs will allow you to increase your knowledge and reduce the risk of financial failure. Successful investors don't become successful overnight; they have endured many challenges along the way yet have managed to find a way through. You can leverage from this learning by understanding what you need to do to reduce your fear of making a financial mistake.

During one of my investment purchases, my mentor assisted me with a concern I had. In a five-minute conversation the result was that I did the deal and saved $20,000 in the process. Had I not had that conversation, I would have pulled out of the deal and missed out on $65,000 of equity built into the deal plus the 20 per cent capital growth we have enjoyed over the past few years.

Here's my tip: to prevent making huge financial mistakes ensure you talk to people who are investors themselves. They can assist you in taking the fear out of investing and fast track you into creating your wealth for your future. The cheapest thing you could ever do is to find a mentor who can help and guide you while you learn the skills of property investing.

Mistake 44 – Falling in love with the property

Many investors forget that purchasing an investment property is all about purchasing a property for someone else to live in (a tenant). They buy the property with their own expectations in mind. They care what the curtains look like and if the kitchen has stainless steel appliances and whether the colour scheme is to their taste. An investment property is just that – an investment property; a means to creating wealth.

Now to be fair, I fell in love with our first investment property. Even though I had just completed a property investment course and understood the concept of falling in love with the numbers first, I couldn't help but be excited about buying my first property. I had spent my working life living from paycheck to paycheck, scratching to pay each bill on time and never managing to get ahead. Sound familiar? When I purchased my first investment property, I was so excited about owning my very own property, I fell in love with it.

The double-storey townhouse was so spacious with a huge living/dining area. It had a spa bath in the main bathroom and a view of the city from the balcony. The kitchen was every woman's dream, more cupboards and bench space than two kitchens combined. It's no secret; I wanted to live in it so the curtains I bought for the property were what I liked in a house. They were thick heavy drapes with a high quality block out to ensure they would help protect against the sun in summer and keep the place warm in winter. I had crappy cheap vertical blinds at home so putting in these beautiful curtains was something I desperately wanted for myself.

I nearly convinced my husband to consider us moving into our first investment property which was brand new, clean, spacious, had stainless steel appliances, a spa bath, ensuite and city views, and rent out our home which was old and in need of major renovation including a new bathroom, laundry, kitchen, cooking appliances, curtains, garage, driveway and repainting. It was a tough decision to make – do we stay or do we go? The numbers encouraged us to stay put.

At the time, I failed to understand that it's the tenant who uses the curtains, not me. In fact our current tenant in that property has been there for a few years. He is a typical single male, untidy and smokes. I am sure he doesn't appreciate the quality and expense of those curtains. I cringe every time I think about it, but he pays the rent every month so I can't complain.

Solution
Focus on the area in which you are purchasing your investment property and speak to local property managers about the sort of things tenants in that area look for when renting. A property manager can give you a wealth of information about what tenants want, so listen closely. If you are purchasing a property in a hot climate, make sure your investment property has air conditioning. If your investment property is targeting families, then a dishwasher and a well-fenced backyard for the children to play in would be sought after. If your investment property is an apartment, then consider balconies and internal laundries. Target properties that tenants like to live in and ensure they have the

features they are looking for. For example, a property with 12-foot ceilings may be nice for you or me to have, but a tenant probably won't care. An air conditioner or dishwasher would be more sought after than high ceilings and an air conditioner and dishwasher would earn you more rent, therefore giving you a better return on your investment. As for my beautiful curtains, well they were a huge expense at the time and earned us no extra rent.... that's right, no extra rent!

So it is really easy to avoid this mistake. Purchase properties that tenants want to live in and try not to care about the curtains. If you are buying your first investment property, quite often the property can highlight the things you do not have where you are living now, as it did for me. It can also be emotional because it is your first transaction.

Here's my tip: stay focused on the bigger picture. You are buying this investment property to create financial wealth for yourself. By doing the homework on what tenants want, you will avoid the emotional roller coaster ride. It does get easier with each additional property purchase you make thereafter. Practice makes perfect.

Mistake 45 – In property investing, no means try again

The word 'no' can stop us in our tracks, but successful people always look for another way. It stems back to our childhood where we have become accustomed to hearing the word 'no'.

As children we always have mum and dad telling us 'no, you can't have that', 'no, don't touch that', no, don't go there' and then we grow up and get a job. We then have our bosses saying 'no, you can't have the day off', 'no, you need to do it this way', and 'no, you can't have that pay rise'.

So it makes sense that we are so easily stopped by the word 'no'. We are conditioned by our environment to accept 'no' as final. Unfortunately it prevents us from moving forward and sometimes causes us to even step back. For example, I knew an investor who was busy looking for cash flow opportunities. He spent many hours researching the websites and speaking to real estate agents in the hope of finding a good cash flow deal.

He found some towns with excellent rental returns and proceeded to put in offers on properties for sale. Each time he put in an offer, the vendors knocked him back and even though he would put forward a counter offer, again his offers were rejected. Having difficulty finding a good deal, he would move on to other areas in search of a cash flow property that allowed him to utilise his limited equity and borrowing position. Again he would put in offers and again they would be rejected. After a while the investor started to feel that investing was too difficult, as he could not negotiate a purchase.

These constant rejections resulted in him losing his confidence. He actually stopped looking for property and putting in offers because he had lost his confidence. A sad state to be in, however many investors suffer the 'no' disease and take it personally. They think that 'no' means there is something wrong with them and they can struggle to get back into the swing of investing as a result.

Solution

It's really important when you receive a 'no' when playing the game of property investing that you do not let it stop you. It's also really important that you do not let it mean that there is something wrong with you or that you are selfish or somehow ridiculous. There is nothing wrong with you and a 'no' does not mean 'no' forever. For example, quite often when negotiating a property purchase, vendors have said 'no' to my offer and then changed their minds down the track when their situation changed.

As an investor you are after the best price you can get. Why pay $20,000 more for something when you do not have to? The purpose of negotiating is to try and save yourself some money; in fact we could save ourselves around 20 per cent throughout our lives if we negotiated or even just asked for what we wanted. A refusal does not have to be a reflection of you as a person. A smart investor always looks for a way around a 'no' to make it a 'yes'. For example, once when I was busy purchasing several investment properties thinking that my finances were all okay, I received a 'no' from my finance broker that I would not be able to purchase all the properties I had negotiated on. He explained how the banks were concerned that I was buying too many in one area in a short space of time. The banks were nervous and felt our property purchases were a high risk.

We were informed that we could purchase four out of the five negotiated opportunities. The broker worked hard to try and get all five loans over the line however the banks continued to say 'no'. He also advised us to take the 'no' as a final 'no' and not rock the boat, as it could jeopardise all the loan applications.

The fifth opportunity was too good to let go, hence we started the ball rolling in search of a 'yes', which brings me to this...

Here's my tip:
If you hit the brick wall, go around it
If you can't go around it, go over it
If you can't go over it, go through it
Never give up on your dreams and never give up on yourself.

With perseverance and thinking outside the square, the result was a 'yes' and we purchased the fifth property. Successful investors do not give up the hunt for the 'yes'. It is quite often the journey traveled that gives you the greatest sense of achievement and learnings. It takes courage and determination to find a way around a situation and convert the 'no' to a 'yes'.

Mistake 46 – It won't happen overnight, but it will happen

An interesting statistic is that only 5 to 12 per cent of the population invests in property. Why does it vary so greatly, I hear you ask? During a boom, every man and his dog wants to get on the bandwagon and try to make a quick buck or two, and when the market is on a downturn, speculators disappear and the real investors stay put – hence the statistics drop to around 5 per cent.

Many investors look for an easy way to make money and don't really consider the long-term benefits. Investing in property is at least a seven to ten-year strategy. This is generally the equivalent of one property cycle, during which the capital value generally doubles. As I prefer to adopt the buy-and-hold strategy, investing for shorter timeframes, I believe, is a waste of time.

In addition to this, some investors do not look at the long-term benefits of cash flow. They only see what the return is today without considering the benefits it will bring tomorrow. For instance, if you receive a 5 per cent return on your investment today, rental increases over time will lead to your investment providing you with a higher income, making the property more cash flow positive. For example, a few years ago we purchased a property for $240,000 which provided us with a rent of $400 per week. Today the same property gives us $600 per week. Another of our properties that we purchased for $216,000 was negatively geared when we bought it, yet today it returns a rent of $355 per week.

Because we planned for the long term then, today we enjoy a property portfolio that has a combination of negatively geared and positive cash flow properties. With rental increases over the years, we now have a cash surplus each month that allows us to put the money towards more property purchases.

Solution
History shows us that property prices double every seven to ten years, so to grow real wealth, holding on for the long term is what successful investors do.

My mother bought a house 20 years ago for $100,000, today it is worth $300,000. At the time she purchased it, it was hard to imagine it would be worth $300,000 in 20 years' time. Even though there may be booms and busts over time, property consistently goes up.

Try and purchase your property investments in a balanced way so that your lifestyle is not greatly impacted. This will eventually make it easy to hold on for the long term and create maximum benefit. Also, when considering a property purchase, use your property analysis software to calculate the income and expenses for today as well as 10 years from now.

We know of an investor who purchased vast tracts of land in the outer areas of a major capital city. He saw something others could not see. He saw the future potential for the land and he acted on his due diligence. Years ago, when he purchased the land, people thought he was mad and that he had made a huge financial mistake.

Today that land is worth millions of dollars and has been subdivided into smaller blocks and become part of a new suburb. He had the foresight to see that the urban sprawl would move out far enough to include his land.

Here's my tip: when looking at purchasing properties, consider the long-term effect of rent on your cash flow. However, do not underestimate the quality of your due diligence because it can give you the edge and provide you with opportunities that many investors would normally miss.

Mistake 47 – Failing to invest in your best asset – YOU!

I have been mentoring clients on property investing for many years and am proud to say that my clients have achieved a high success rate in sourcing and purchasing their first, and sometimes second and third, investment properties while on our programs.

Yet many investors feel that having a coach or mentor to guide them in their property investing journey is an unnecessary expense. They believe they can learn it all by themselves, making their own mistakes along the way. The problem with this approach is that when investing in property you are dealing with big-dollar purchases that can turn out to be high risk if you do not have a proper understanding of the pitfalls.

You may think that it can't be that hard to buy an investment property. What I can say from bitter experience is that it's a case of "what you don't know that you don't know". By investing in yourself you can discover the things that you "don't know that you don't know" about buying an investment property. I have invested a lot of time and money in educating myself, not only in property but in the reasons why I had not considered investing in property in the first place.

If someone had said to me a few years ago that I would be spending a lot of my time and money on property education and mentors, I would have told them they were crazy. I now realise that spending hundreds of thousands of dollars buying investment property with very little education or understanding of what I was doing would have been the crazy thing to do. I learnt that I needed to invest in myself before I began investing in property.

Over the years I have discovered that there are two major components to investing in yourself. The first component is that of investor mindset and the other is the 'nuts and bolts' of whatever you are investing in. The two are inextricably linked and therefore cannot be done in isolation. Mindset is by far the most important and is about understanding yourself and why you do or don't invest. The 'nuts and bolts' of property education is about understanding the "how to" of successful property investing.

Back in my 'rat race' days, I worked with someone who decided to get into property investing and purchased what he thought was a good property. As I was also into investing, we would regularly chat about his purchase and how he was going with it. The more he told me the more I realised that his investment choice was not really a good financial decision, as he had paid more for the property than it was worth. When I made a few suggestions, including a couple of courses for him to do, his reaction was to say that it wasn't necessary. If he had been trained in how to research a property purchase correctly, his mistake could have been avoided.

It fascinates me that people will buy a $300,000 property with very little research, guidance, knowledge or understanding of how to do it yet they will spend weeks researching, analysing, haggling, reviewing, talking and reading magazines before they will purchase a new $30,000 car or a new $6000 home theatre system.

Solution
Over the years, I have come to realise that the reason why I didn't invest in property before was due to my small minded, negative attitude towards wealth and those who had it. I believed I needed money to make money and since we didn't have it, that I was not likely to ever have it.

Then the breakthrough came. I call it an 'Aha moment' (An 'Aha moment' is when you learn something new and didn't realise the impact it would have on you). For me this moment occurred during my first property seminar when I realised that 90 per cent of the reason why I hadn't commenced investing before was because of my negative mindset. I also learned that not all debt was bad and that I could create massive wealth using someone else's money – wow, did that blow my mind!

This seminar was my springboard into property investing and whetted my appetite and thirst for obtaining more knowledge. I wanted to understand more and more about what made property investing tick. This led me to more courses and a greater understanding of how the rich create wealth and why the poor have no idea.

What I also realised was that not only is an education vital to being a successful property investor but having someone mentor me through each stage was also extremely important to avoiding making big and costly mistakes. Having an experienced mentor (a successful property investor in their own right) by my side, holding my hand throughout the process, taught me how to succeed without fear.

If you have been to the seminars, read the books, magazines and have been thinking and talking about investing in property for a long time and yet have still not purchased a property, then it's probably because you haven't really invested in yourself.

Here's my tip: seek out an experienced mentor who has the following attributes:

- has 10 or more investment properties themselves;
- will educate and work with you to achieve your financial goals;
- has achieved what it is that you want to achieve;
- does not try to sell you properties (i.e., doesn't have a vested interest in the outcome);

- has years of experience in property investing; and
- will guide you from personal experience rather than theory.

Remember, investing in property without investing in yourself is gambling and we all know where that leads to.

Conclusion

Making mistakes is all part of life and we generally learn the most when we personally experience a situation and overcome it. We also have the ability to learn from other people's mistakes without having to discover them all by ourselves. I would not have gained the knowledge I have today if it had not been for the mistakes I have made along the way. My critical moments in life have been my greatest discoveries. I have no doubt that I could have fast tracked my discoveries by learning from other people's mistakes and not from my own.

As I am writing this page, it allows me to realise how far I have come. Today, I can honestly say that I have achieved the impossible and it scares me to think what I will achieve in the next five to ten years. As a '30-something' year old, the one thing I do know is that my life is the result of getting off my backside and having a go. I have learnt to let go of my fears and move forward.

I watched a movie the other night called 'Last Holiday', starring Queen Latifah. It was a comedy with a fantastic message. Without giving the whole plot away, she was told she had three weeks left to live. How she chose to live out her final days was hilarious. One thing she did do was live life fully. In writing a letter containing her final wishes, she requested to be cremated as she felt she had "lived her life in a box and didn't want to be buried in one". It really hit home to me how incredibly true that statement is. I know myself that I on many occasions stopped or held myself back as a result of my fears. Sometimes my concerns about making a mistake and therefore looking bad or feeling like an idiot caused me to not do anything. At times I even felt helpless and hopeless. I felt like I had no future and drifted from day to day.

The trials and tribulations of my childhood plagued me in my younger years (not that I am that old now) and caused me to think and feel 'average'. I would never believe that good things would happen to me, they only happened to those who were 'lucky' or 'smart' or 'beautiful' or 'rich', and not me. I always blamed others for my misfortunes in life and on occasions would even yell at God for giving me such a 'stuffed up life and family'. Thank goodness I wasn't listened to, as I am so grateful to all who are in my life (past and present).

It wasn't until the end of my 20s that life (or should I say my thinking) started to change. It became a natural transition once I started to become accountable for my actions and give up blaming the world for my 'shitty' life. Being accountable led me to have a different view of the world, it's as if someone took off the rose coloured glasses and now I am seeing the world in techno colour.

Our wealth creation journey has been truly amazing and even though I am optimistic about life, I am still a realist. When it comes to property investing I continue to focus on the numbers and avoid making any huge mistakes. If you have taken on creating wealth through property investing or are a beginner and want to get started, you may want to consider not telling the world what you are embarking on to avoid the negative talk and backlash you may get from people. I know we quickly learnt this lesson. It wasn't worth talking to the uninitiated about investing, as they were generally coming from a place of fear and a lack of knowledge. The solution is to try and find like-minded people who share the same interest – property. In your circle of friends and family, there will be those you talk to about property and those you don't. It's just the way things are. Try and understand that not everyone is as passionate about wealth creation as you are. Friends and family may be travelling a different journey and the path you are on may not necessarily work for them.

Outside of your social circle, look for mentors and/or coaches who can work with you or groups that provide education and networking and make sure they are not just trying to sell you an investment property. This experience may help to fast track your investing experience as well as overcome any hurdles you may face along the way.

If you are a beginner, it's especially important in the game of property investing to not fall in love with a property as I did. My solution was to stay focused on the numbers. When you fully understand the cost of investing and how negative gearing impacts your back pocket, it does make it easier to view each investment as a business and be able to give up the emotional attachment. As a rule of thumb, it is generally easier for men to focus on the numbers while we women tend to care about how the property looks. We are 'right brain' (creative) and men are 'left brain' (logical) therefore men are genetically designed to focus on the mechanics or technical aspects of investing – well that's my excuse and I am sticking to it! I am sure that Ed would like to add in here that women are genetically designed to shop and I have no intention of educating him to think any other way.

When it comes to investing, Ed is usually the one who looks at all the details, especially when it comes to finance. I enjoy the detail when it comes to undertaking all the research for an area or property but I generally prefer to deal with 'concepts', 'strategies' and 'big picture' stuff. When it came to the mistake of 'hitting the financial brick wall', it caught both of us unaware. Although painful at the time, we learnt a new strategy which enabled us to move forward and overcome this mistake.

The solution to balancing your portfolio is really like riding a bike. You don't want to tip too far one way as you will fall over. Keeping the portfolio in balance, between negative gearing and cash flow, allows you to enjoy the ride and fast track you from A to B. By keeping your balance, the journey is smoother and you are more likely to overcome any obstacles along the way. After all, no one likes to ride a bike leaning to one side.

Although we hear a great deal about negative gearing, it is really important to consider your cash flow. As for Ed and I, purchasing several cash flow positive properties really made a huge difference to the amount of money coming out of our pockets each week. As a result of the cash flow properties, we enjoy a cash surplus each month. You will hear from people who believe that 'negative gearing' is the way to go when creating your wealth or that 'positive cash flow' is the only way. Well, like everything else in life, I believe the best method is everything in 'moderation' or 'balance'. Therefore I prefer both options as I have personally experienced the impacts of not following the 'balanced' strategy. The same can be said when conducting your due diligence. Always keep your numbers balanced and ensure your due diligence is conducted in a balanced way. By that I mean it's important to go with what your research is telling you and not to listen solely to what people may tell you, such as the real estate agent. They are a wealth of information and I have met some fantastic agents over the years, however it is important to understand what drives them – a commission!

When anyone has a vested financial interest in the outcome, be wary. I learnt this the hard way by not cross-referencing what the agent had told me. Had I done my homework properly and not cut corners, I would not have purchased our eighth property. Anyway, it's history now as we have sold it. I will never solely listen to anyone again when making my property purchases. I will always double-check the facts from other sources to ensure I minimise the chance of making that mistake in the future. This leads me to say how important it is to follow a process. At the end of the day, property investing is simple – investing in anything is a step-by-step process. It takes some work yet the results can be fantastic. If you leave out a step, it's more than likely things will go haywire. A step-by-step process coupled with your clear goals creates a powerful combination for getting you going. To invest you need to have a 'why', which is the reason or the driving force for doing something. The 'how' is usually the process you follow to achieve your 'why'. Setting goals gives you something to aim for – the 'why', while the step-by-step process is the plan – the 'how'.

The third part of being a successful property investor is that you need to have passion. Passion helps you to keep going when there are obstacles in your way. Let's face it, if we went through life with no challenges, life would be rather boring. Don't be afraid to make mistakes but do try and consider your exit strategy as a means for lowering the risk. There is no point going bankrupt trying to get rich.

'Why' + 'How' + 'Passion' = Success

I have read a book called "Good to Great" by Jim Collins and in the book he tells the story of the Fox and the Hedgehog. The story talks about the fox being the type of person who is *"scattered or diffused moving on many levels and always looking for the next biggest thing. Foxes pursue many ends at the same time and see the world in all its complexity... (however) never integrating their thinking into one overall concept or unifying vision. Hedgehogs, on the other hand, simplify a complex world into a single organising idea, a basic principle or concept that unifies and guides everything. It doesn't matter how complex the world, a Hedgehog reduces all challenges and dilemmas to simple – indeed almost simplistic – Hedgehog ideas. Hedgehogs see what is essential and ignore the rest".*

Being the Hedgehog has allowed Ed and I to build a multi-million dollar property portfolio and we have been able to achieve this through the guidance of our coaches and mentors. This guidance has fast tracked our education without having to personally experience all the possible challenges that occur when creating wealth. Although we have made our fair share of mistakes, the education we have received over the years, and will continue to seek, not only grows us wealth but it also grows and expands our spirit. The best fun is not the end result of owning many properties but more the journey we travelled to achieve it. Our partnership has grown stronger, the friendships we have made along the way have been amazing and the opportunities we have been granted are beyond our wildest dreams. I am grateful to the universe for the opportunity to write this book and I look forward to writing more in my lifetime. My intention is to share with the world my knowledge and experience on how to create real wealth in all areas of our lives.

Part 6 – Useful Resources

Now what? Where to from here? You have read this book and are thinking 'what next'? Being the avid educator I am, the following pages will provide you with some useful information to assist you with your property investing. I have also included a budget planner, which is a great place for you to start. I cannot stress enough the importance of completing a budget to allow you to fully understand your financial position. Without it, you are flying blind or, as we like to say, 'gambling' with your money.

As an investor myself I usually like to follow a step-by-step process. That way it keeps life simple and reduces any risk of making a mistake. Property investing is very easy but it's the learning that takes time and energy. Therefore it's important you put into practice the things that you learn to gain greater momentum in life. This applies to everything you do. You can't drive a car without practice and the same can be said about property investing – you need to practice.

To help you practice, I have included a 'simple process' for you to follow so that you can take some action.

17 critical steps to property investing

Step 1	Build a team of experts to support you
Step 2	Establish your borrowing position
Step 3	Establish the right entity to buy your property in
Step 4	Establish the right buying strategy
Step 5	Establish your buying rules
Step 6	Find the property
Step 7	Crunch the numbers
Step 8	Make an offer
Step 9	Obtain a market rental appraisal
Step 10	Negotiate the price
Step 11	Organise inspections
Step 12	Apply for finance
Step 13	Arrange insurance
Step 14	Settlement period
Step 15	Depreciation schedule
Step 16	Exit strategy
Step 17	Celebrate

Step 1: Build a team of experts to support you

You can't be an expert at everything and when buying property you are dealing in big dollars, therefore finding the right expert(s) to support you in making your decisions is extremely important. Examples of the type of expert you will need to have on your team include a solicitor, accountant, finance broker, property coach/mentor, property manager, valuer, quantity surveyor and insurance broker.

Make sure the experts you choose are active property investors themselves and if not, seek out experts who are. If you choose an expert who is not a property investor, then expect to make mistakes and/or minimise instead of maximise the return on your investment.

Step 2: Establish your borrowing position

Contact your bank or finance broker and ask them for an assessment of your borrowing position. In other words, find out what your borrowing risk profile is with the bank, how much you can borrow, what your available equity is, what your serviceability profile is and what you can do to improve all of the above. Remember, you want to maximise your borrowing potential. Every borrowed dollar at 7.5 per cent interest that returns 15 per cent or more puts money into your pocket.

Don't stop at one bank. Every bank has different borrowing rules for lenders. You will get a different story at each bank. Try both traditional and non-traditional banks. You may be surprised at the difference.

Knowing your borrowing position and what you can do to improve it helps you to plan and work out the type, number and profile of the properties you can afford to buy.

Don't forget to complete your budget.

Step 3: Establish the right entity to buy your property in

Now that you have established your borrowing position, the question you will next face is what entity you should purchase the investment property in. Should it be in your own name, your spouse's, child's or partner's name. Or should it be in a trust (hybrid, discretionary or unit trust), a company or a combination of the above? Also, how many properties should you purchase in the one entity and why? How should you structure the purchase to provide maximum asset protection while at the same time providing you with maximum leverage, minimum tax and the best return on your investment?

Choosing the wrong entity could have significant adverse tax implications for you, so make sure you discuss this with your accountant and solicitor.

It is important that you work out the right buying entity before you purchase a property, as you won't be able to change it later on without attracting significant additional costs, including the dreaded stamp duty.

Step 4: Establish the right buying strategy

Now that you know your financial buying position, have found the appropriate experts to support you, and the right entity to purchase the property in, the next big question is what kind of property should you buy? Should it be a capital growth (often negatively geared), cash flow neutral, positively geared or a cash flow positive property? What kind of return do you need to get from the property in order to sustain it and/or your lifestyle? Can you afford to be funding the balance of a negatively geared property out of your own pocket if there is a shortfall between the rent and expenses? If so, how much and for how long?

It is extremely important that you consider your lifestyle when creating your buying strategy because if buying properties results in you not being able to afford to go out to dinner or the movies, how long do you think you will put up with it? Experience suggests about two years at the most, you'll then sell up, lose money and label property investing a mug's game.

Looking for a balanced buying strategy that does not adversely impact on your lifestyle is what long term property investors strive for. Spend some serious time up front with your property mentor/coach developing your buying strategy, you won't regret it.

Step 5: Establish your buying rules

Having established your financial position, built your team of experts, established your buying entity and developed a buying strategy that will suit your lifestyle, it is now time to develop buying rules that support your buying strategy.

Buying rules will help you focus your search on properties that fit your buying strategy and stop you from diverting your property search to all ends of the globe. Typical questions you should ask yourself when establishing your buying rules are:

- What kind of properties should you purchase – houses, units, townhouses or apartments?
- How many bedrooms should it have – one, two, three or more?
- Should it have a rumpus room, and/or an alfresco entertainment area?
- Should it have a single or double garage or none at all?
- Should it have one, two or more bathrooms?
- Should it be single level or multiple levels?
- If apartments are the focus of your search, what should the maximum number of apartments be in the development?
- Where should you focus your property search – locally, interstate or overseas?
- What yield should the property provide? How much are you prepared to spend on the property?
- Should you buy old or new properties?
- Should the properties be in a capital city or in the country?
- Should the property have a pool?
- Should the property have air conditioning?
- Do you want to add value to the property later on and if so, how?
- Should it be near schools, public transport and major roads? If so, how far should you have to travel to get to them?
- How far (driving/flying time) should it be from the nearest major or capital city?
- Should there be an airport/train station nearby? If so, how far should it be from the property?
- Should it be near major shopping centres, cafes, restaurants etc.?
- What should the percentage of renters be in the area?

- What should the target vacancy rate be in the focus area?
- If the focus is on capital growth, what should the capital growth be?
- Should you buy by private treaty or at auction?

Your buying rules may change from property purchase to property purchase because your borrowing capacity may have changed. Your property coach/mentor can assist you in developing these rules.

Once your buying rules have been established, stick to them for the purchase at hand.

Buying rules

		Location List 2-3 areas that suit your requirements	Price Range	Property Type (house, unit etc.)	Positive Cash Flow Required ($)	Minimum Capital Growth Required (%)
Cash Flow	1					
	2					
	3					

Capital Growth	1					
	2					
	3					

Step 6: Find the property

Having completed steps 1 to 5, it is now time to purchase the property. The first step is to select three areas of buying interest that relate to your strategy (i.e. cash flow or capital growth). This will need to involve assistance from reputable property research analysts which your property coach/mentor can assist you in finding.

Use the many internet property websites available as a means of finding properties in your search areas and then use the buying rules you have established to hone in on the right property. Again, your property coach/mentor can assist you in identifying and gaining best use of these websites.

Contact three property managers in your search area and ask them what tenants are looking for when looking for a rental property. This will help with selecting a property that tenants want to live in. Use the same property managers to assist you to assess the vacancy rate in the area.

You could also contact three real estate agents in your nominated search area, give them an outline of your buying rules and ask them to contact you with any properties that fit the property profile you are looking for. This can save you heaps of search time, but make sure you convince them that you are serious about buying a property as this will really get their attention.

Look for distressed sellers for potential discount opportunities.

Step 7: Crunch the numbers

Remember the property investor's golden rule… "Fall in love with the deal not the property". In order to do this you will need to analyse the property financials to ensure the property fits your buying strategy.

This can be done quickly by using reputable property analysis software. The software will allow you to put in all the purchasing costs and property expenses and come up with a net weekly after or pre-tax loss or income from the property. If the property doesn't quite fit your buying rules at the price being asked by the vendor, you can then manipulate the purchase price figure in the software until you get a scenario that has the deal stacking up to your required buying rule. This then becomes your upper price for negotiating the deal.

Your property coach/mentor will be able to advise you on software and assist you in crunching the numbers. Beware that some property analysis software, especially if offered by vested interest developers, can be misleading.

Step 8: Make an offer

When you have found the investment property you are interested in buying and the numbers work for you, put in an offer in writing. This must be done quickly. Add "subject to" clauses in the contract/agreement under 'Special Conditions' and put in your offer quickly to make sure another buyer does not gazump you. This should be done even if you haven't quite completed your "due diligence" checks on the property.

The purpose of the "subject to" clauses is to conditionally purchase the property so that you have the time to complete your "due diligence" without feeling that you are under pressure from other buyers. Make sure you give yourself plenty of time in the "subject to" clauses to allow you to complete your "due diligence" investigations. If the vendor accepts your conditional offer, then the property is withdrawn from the market until such time as the "subject to" clause timeframe expires or the buyer decides to purchase the property unconditionally.

Step 9: Obtain a market rental appraisal

It's important that while you have the property off the market you ask the property manager to put their rental appraisal in writing. You want to find out as part of your 'due diligence' how much your chosen property will rent for. This allows you, when crunching the numbers, to work out how much it will either cost you per week (if negatively geared) or how much it will add to your pocket per week (if cash flow positive).

Having the appraisal in writing gives you confidence that the expected rental income is accurate enough to assist you in making your financial decision as to whether the investment property will work for you. Obtaining a market rental appraisal from three different property managers will give you an excellent idea of the market for your selected property purchase.

Step 10: Negotiate the price

You don't always have to pay a vendor's asking price to purchase an investment property. Experience says that many vendors are prepared to accept less than what they are asking for, so as a way of saving yourself thousands of dollars always offer less. The money you save as a result of your negotiations is money in your pocket rather than the vendor's.

As a guide, in a booming market seek to achieve a 5 to 10 per cent discount, in a flat market aim for a 10 to 15 per cent discount and in a bust market aim to achieve 20 per cent plus as a discount off the sale price.
If you can't achieve these amounts, at least aim to obtain a discount as every dollar you save goes into your pocket. Continue to negotiate until the contract is accepted or rejected.

Step 11: Organise inspections

Inspections are an important part of conducting your 'due diligence' as it allows you to ascertain the true condition of the property. Sometimes a physical inspection of a property may not alert you to what hides underneath. Pest and building inspections, where required, allow you to bring in the experts to review the property in detail. This is especially important when dealing with old properties.

A building inspection will check the roof cavity, under the house (if on stumps) and areas that you may not consider inspecting. Should the report come back with defects, this now gives you the opportunity to go back to the vendor to either seek compensation for the cost of repairs or you are well within your rights to ask them to rectify areas of concern.

Same can be done with the pest inspection. If termites are found on the property (whether in the house or outside), you can ask the vendor to compensate you by reducing the price further or have them rectify the matter to your satisfaction.

Including clauses in your contract that allow you access to the property to conduct your inspections can save you thousands in future costs and more importantly, future headaches.

Step 12: Apply for finance

Although you would have sorted out your borrowing capacity as part of the initial process, it is now time to make a formal application for finance. One of your clauses should be a 'subject to finance' clause which gives you time to obtain the finance from your bank or broker.

Try to allow as much time for finance as possible, as experience shows that there are usually delays of one kind or another. Allowing yourself more time for finance makes the process smoother and gives you greater peace of mind.

Again from experience, there is nothing worse than being charged interest by the vendor because you failed to meet the finance deadline. Failing to meet the deadline can occur for many reasons, including documents not being received by either party, solicitors forgetting to contact your bank, bank valuers being too busy and therefore held up in viewing the property, parts of your finance application being incomplete, bank solicitors requiring more information or it could be a combination of the above. It's not about blaming the bank. By being proactive you can buy yourself time to sort things out. Once finance and other conditions are met, go unconditional.

Step 13: Arrange insurance

As part of your finance approval, your bank will require that you obtain building insurance. This is an opportune time to arrange for house, contents and landlords insurance before the tenant moves in. Remember to include contents insurance as it covers carpets and curtains. The tenant should also have contents insurance to cover their furniture.

About 60 per cent of landlords do not have landlords insurance. The cheapest way to lower your risk as an investor is through landlords insurance. A good landlords insurance policy (you must read the inclusions in the policy) will cover you for loss of rent for a set number of weeks/months if the tenant cannot pay or leaves without paying rent, damage to the property and rent while the damage is being fixed, failure to pay rent during eviction and any court costs should you need to take your tenant to court. The policy will generally require that losses are extracted from bond monies before the insurance company commences paying.

Of course you have the bond at your disposal should monies be owed to you by the tenant, however what if the damage costs more than the bond?

Make sure you check what the inclusions are in the policy. As a rule of thumb when it comes to insurance, if you pay peanuts you will get monkeys. Also, check what the excesses are on each item.

Step 14: Settlement period

Once the contract has gone unconditional, your finance is sorted and you are waiting to take possession of the property, use this time during the settlement period to interview three property managers. When you find a good property manager, get them to advertise your property and find you a tenant. Check with your accountant that the tax deductibility of the interest commences when you commence advertising the property for rent.

Your settlement period could be a few weeks or a few months (depending on conditions or state of purchase) so use the time to find a tenant. Any savvy investor will always seek to have a tenant moving into their property shortly after settlement.

You can either revisit the property managers that gave you a rental appraisal or seek out others. Experience has shown that property managers who manage more than 200 properties at a time will be ineffective in looking after your investment. Your property mentor/coach should be able to provide you with questions to ask property managers when you interview them. Inexperienced or overworked property managers will result in lack of attention to your property, which in turn will lead to the property being allowed to "run down".

At the beginning of the tenancy have your property manager conduct a complete and thorough inspection of the property taking lots of photos inside and out for their records.

Step 15: Depreciation schedule

Many investors do not realise that a quantity surveyor is the only person the Australian Tax Office recognises as being qualified to provide you with a tax depreciation schedule. Accountants are not qualified to provide the cost of installation of depreciable items, hence many investors miss out on valuable tax-deductible depreciation benefits.

Once you have possession of the property, organise for a quantity surveyor to assess your property and provide you with a depreciation schedule. This is then given to your accountant who will include the depreciable amounts in your tax return calculations. The quantity surveyors fees are also tax deductible.

Step 16: Exit strategy

What is your exit strategy for your new property purchase? Will you buy and hold for the long term or will you sell in the short term? Will you add value to the property through renovation, subdivision or development? When will you revalue the property and use the equity to purchase the next property?

When we purchase property we usually have a very good idea of what we plan to do with it before we buy. This allows us to plan for any obstacles we may come across. We have, on occasions, also changed our minds and decided to add value or sell as a result. As we constantly review our position and as circumstances change, we try to plan ahead as best we can as part of our exit strategy.

Step 17: Celebrate

It is always important to celebrate your achievements; it becomes all the more worthwhile. Reward yourself with a dinner at a fancy restaurant or that iPod you have been wanting. Keep your rewards manageable so you don't break the bank, yet allow yourself to enjoy the fruits of your efforts.

Budget Planner

INCOME	MONTHLY	ANNUALLY
Salary		
Bonuses		
Investment income (interest, rent, dividends)		
Allowances		
Other		
TOTAL INCOME		

EXPENSES	MONTHLY	ANNUALLY
(a) LOANS		
Mortgage (or rent paid)		
Interest payments on investments		
Car loan		
Other loan		
Credit card 1		
Credit card 2		
Store card		
Other		
TOTAL		

(b) LIVING EXPENSES	MONTHLY	ANNUALLY
Home maintenance		
Rates and levies (council, water)		
Phone (rental, service and calls)		
Mobile phone		
Utilities (gas, electricity)		
Food/groceries/household		
Alcohol		
Cigarettes		
Medical and pharmaceuticals		
Alternative medicine		
Wardrobe (clothes, shoes, bags etc.)		

Child care		
School fees		
Pay TV		
Personal education / courses		
Pets (food, vet care etc.)		
Household purchases (eg. furniture, appliances etc.)		
Household improvements (eg. carpet, curtains etc.)		
Other		
TOTAL		

(c) VEHICLE / TRANSPORT	MONTHLY	ANNUALLY
Registration		
Maintenance / repairs		
Fuel		
Taxis		
Public transport fares		
Parking		
TOTAL		

(d) INSURANCE	MONTHLY	ANNUALLY
Home and contents		
Life / income protection		
Car		
Boat / trailer/ motorcycle/ caravan		
Health		
Business		
Superannuation		
Travel		
Other		
TOTAL		

(e) LEISURE / ENTERTAINMENT	MONTHLY	ANNUALLY
Holidays		
Restaurants		
Outings / takeaways		
Sports /hobbies/ memberships		
Newspaper /magazines including subscriptions		
Books /CDs/ DVDs etc.		
Computer equipment		
Gifts		
Other		
Any other expenses		
TOTAL	$	$

TOTAL EXPENSES (Add A, B, C, D and E)	$	$
INCOME MINUS EXPENSES = disposable income	$	$

10 keys to research

Research, or 'due diligence' as we like to call it, plays a significant role in the outcome of property investing. If you get it right, the result is often a fabulous investment property, but if you get it wrong it can cost you dearly. There are a number of areas you need to consider when conducting your due diligence.

1. Demographics

This tells you what the break-up of the population is for your specific area of interest. For example, you want to know how many people in a suburb or town rent so that you can ascertain whether there is a high enough number of people to rent your investment property to. There is no point buying an investment property if there is no one to rent it from you. You also want to know what type of people live in the area you are buying in, such as single people, couples, families etc. This will assist with the type of property you buy and tailor your investment purchase to the market. For example, if the majority of people living in a particular area are single, then small units or one or two-bedroom apartments may be a more appropriate investment than a four-bedroom house.

2. Area profile

What is it about your selected area that makes people want to live there? Have a look at what the area has to offer, such as lifestyle, restaurants, shopping, medical, schools, sea/beach etc. Try and ascertain what makes your selected area more preferred than a neighbouring suburb or town. If the area is sought after, this helps to ensure your investment property is always rented due to people wanting to live in that particular suburb or town.

3. Population and growth

You want to know more about the population of the selected suburb or town for two reasons. One, it's vital that there are enough people living there, and two, that the population is growing. It is of particular interest to know how many people are living in the area, especially when you are buying in regional areas. Reason being that smaller towns have fewer people living in them, therefore a smaller market of renters is available to rent your property. You do not want your investment property remaining vacant for long periods of time, so minimise this risk by selecting areas with larger populations.

On the second point, population growth indicates if there are more people moving into the area and the more people, the bigger the market of renters to rent your investment property. There are many reports available in newspapers and magazines, which often outline population movements and forecasts. These reports can be very useful to an investor.

4. Sales data and history

As part of your research, you want to learn more about the number of property sales that have occurred over the past three months. If you have found a property you are interested in, you want to investigate what other similar properties have sold for. The simple way is to ask the real estate agent. May I also suggest that you not limit yourself to one agent and go as far as asking other real estate agents from other agencies. Looking for sales data on similar properties helps to ascertain if you are paying fair market value or if you are paying too much/too little for the property. The sales history can also give you an idea of demand for the area and its growth.

5. Median house/unit price

In conjunction with sales data, have a look at what the median house price is in the area. As a rule of thumb, I generally like to purchase property at around the median house price. Why, I hear you ask? It's because this forms part of our risk mitigation strategy. We want to make sure the properties we purchase are in the price range that most people can afford to buy (should we want to sell) and rent our property. For example, if the median house price for an area is $320,000, purchasing a house for $550,000 would be above median, hence limiting the number of people that may be able to afford to rent your property.

6. Capital growth statistics

Capital growth data provides an investor a guide to what the capital growth for the area has been in the past and what it may be in the future. Now, no one has a crystal ball, however if the experts have studied all the key factors which cause capital growth then it can be used as a guide for selecting an area to invest in. History is often a good guide for predicting the future. I like to examine the capital growth of an area for the past twelve months, five years and then ten years. If the growth has been fairly consistent over time, this gives me confidence of its future predicted growth.

7. Rental data and vacancy rates

Data can be obtained from rental managers in your selected area or town. You want to find out the number of properties currently up for rent. How long does it take to rent a property? Has the rent increased over the past two years? How many properties do the rental agents manage? Obtaining this information is usually a case of asking the local property managers in the area. They are generally a wealth of information and can provide you with an excellent understanding of the rental market. Your main question should be regarding vacancy rates. You want to make sure that vacancy rates are low. Anything above 5 per cent can result in your property being vacant for up to four weeks or more. As a rule of thumb, vacancy rates of 3 per cent or less are ideal.

8. Infrastructure, employment and business

These are all major parts to your due diligence. Try and find out what infrastructure exists in the area or town. Infrastructure generally creates employment and can encourage people to want to live in the area. For example, does the area have easy access by road, rail or bus? Are there major projects going on to build new motorways or upgrade existing roads? Are there schools and universities in the vicinity? How about a hospital, shopping centre/complex or restaurants? Is there an airport nearby? What about a designated industrial/commercial area? These are all important questions you need to answer for the particular location you are looking at. It indicates what employment exists locally and if it is growing. It all adds to the sustainability of the area, which in turn protects your asset by providing a ready market of renters in need of rental accommodation.

9. Council

It pays to look at local council websites as they are a wealth of information and tell you what is going on in the area. Council websites can also be a great source for obtaining information on demographics and future projections.

10. Property management

Property managers are an excellent source of information when looking for a potential investment property to purchase. They deal with tenants on a daily basis and know what rents well in the area and what is sought after by tenants. When researching an area, speak to the local property managers and seek their opinion on what tenants want. The best part about property managers is that they do not play a role in the sale of any property, hence they are more impartial in the advice they give. Their objective is to manage properties that are sought after by tenants and do not require constant maintenance.

Recommended reading

Title	Author
Good to Great	Jim Collins
The Intelligent Investor	Benjamin Graham
The Millionaire Mind	Thomas J. Stanley, Ph.D.
The Millionaire Next Door	Thomas J. Stanley, Ph.D.
Rich Dad, Poor Dad	Robert Kiyosaki
Rich Dad's Who Took My Money?	Robert Kiyosaki
Cashflow Quadrant: Rich Dad's Guide to Financial Freedom	Robert Kiyosaki
Rich Dad's Prophecy	Robert Kiyosaki
Why We Want You To Be Rich	Robert Kiyosaki / Donald Trump
The Richest Man in Babylon	George S. Clason
Think and Grow Rich	Napoleon Hill
As a Man Thinketh	James Allen
The Science to Getting Rich	Wallace D. Wattles
The Alchemist	Paulo Coelho
Chicken Soup for the Soul Series	Mark Victor Hansen and Jack Canfield
The One Minute Millionaire	Mark Victor Hansen
Awaken the Giant Within	Anthony Robbins

The Trick to Money is Having Some!	Stuart Wilde
The Secret	Rhonda Byrne
The Power of Positive Thinking	Norman Vincent Peale
The 7 Habits of Highly Effective People	Stephen Covey
Turning Passions into Profits	Christopher Howard
You Can Have an Amazing Life in Just 60 Days	Dr John Demartini

Suggested websites

There are a number of very useful websites for conducting your research. When looking at a particular area or town, I always look at the website for the local council in that particular area as well as the state council. Below is a list of some of the main websites I have used over the years.

Real Estate Institutes
Australia - www.reia.com.au
NSW - www.reinsw.com.au
WA - www.reiwa.com.au
QLD - www.reiq.com.au
VIC - www.reiv.com.au
SA - www.reisa.com.au

Offices of State Revenue
ACT - www.revenue.act.gov.au
SA - www.revenuesa.sa.gov.au
QLD- www.osr.qld.gov.au
WA - www.dtf.wa.gov.au/cms/osr_index.asp
NSW - www.osr.nsw.gov.au
VIC- www.sro.vic.gov.au

State Councils
Perth City Council - www.cityofperth.wa.gov.au
Adelaide City Council - www.adelaidecitycouncil.com
Sydney City Council - www.cityofsydney.nsw.gov.au
Melbourne City Council - www.melbourne.vic.gov.au
Brisbane City Council - www.brisbane.qld.gov.au

Research
www.homepriceguide.com.au
www.bisshrapnel.com.au
www.residex.com.au
www.midwoodaustralia.com
www.rpdata.net.au
www.matusik.com.au

Government Departments
Australian Bureau of Statistics - www.abs.gov.au
Australian Tax Office (ATO) - www.ato.gov.au
Dept of Environment and Heritage - www.environment.gov.au

Finding Properties
www.realestate.com.au
www.domain.com.au

Glossary of terms

Appraisal/valu ation	A written report of the estimated value of a property, usually prepared by a valuer.
Body corporate	An administrative body made up of all the owners within a group of units or apartments of a strata building. The owners elect a committee which handles administration and upkeep of the site.
Capital gain	The amount by which your property has increased relative to what you paid for it. Simplistically, if you bought a property for $200,000 and it's now worth $350,000, you've made a capital gain of $150,000.
Cash flow positive	You have a cash flow positive investment if the incomings are more than your outgoings after tax deductible items have been claimed. You receive more rent than your mortgage repayments, plus you are still ahead after taking into account items such as interest on the loan, maintenance, insurance, land tax, rates etc.
CGT (capital gains tax)	This is the tax you pay when you sell an investment property if you have made a profit.

Conditional The status of an agreement for sale and purchase which is subject to specified conditions to be satisfied to make it binding.

Due diligence The process by which careful consideration of every aspect of a proposed asset purchase or lease is reviewed, including in-depth financial, legal and physical investigation. Because the purchase or lease of an investment property can be complex, sale and purchase agreements and lease agreements are often conditional upon the completion of due diligence within a specified period to the satisfaction of the purchaser or prospective lessee.

Equity The amount of an asset actually owned. Equity is the difference between the market value of the property and the amount still owed on its mortgage. If your home is worth $400,000 and you owe $150,000, then you have equity of $250,000.

Fixed rates Where the home loan is locked in at a specific mortgage, not paying anything off the principal or amount owing.

Freehold Property held as freehold is often referred to as an estate in Fee Simple. It is the interest in land having the greatest rights of use and enjoyment allowed by law and the widest power of disposal or alienation. All other forms of tenure are created out of a freehold or fee simple.

Joint tenants	Each owner has equal shares and rights in the property.
Lease	A contract granting a right to exclusive possession of real property for a definite period.
Leasehold	An estate or interest in the land defined by a lease contract for a specific period and usually for the payment of rent. The lease transfers the rights of occupation of the property to the lessee who is often subject to covenants as to use, term and rental etc.
Leverage	The degree to which an investor is using borrowed funds.
LMI (lenders mortgage insurance)	It is an insurance policy designed to protect the lender against you defaulting on your loan repayments. It is protection for the lender, not the borrower. If you default on your loan and the lender is forced to sell the property to retrieve its funds, the insurance pays the balance if the amount of funds received is less than the original loan amount. The insurance company then has legal rights to pursue the borrower to recoup these funds. Usually, in loans greater than 80 per cent of the value of the security, the borrower pays the mortgage insurance premium.

LOC (line of credit)	A facility available from financial institutions that give you a credit limit that you can draw down at any time.
LVR (loan-to-value ratio)	This is the measure of the amount of the loan compared to the value of the property. To calculate it, divide the loan amount by the value of the property then multiply by 100 to get a percentage. Banks and financial institutions use this as a measure of whether you can afford the loan.
Median	The median house price is the middle price of all sales recorded in a particular suburb, postcode, city or state. For example, if there were 100 sales in a particular suburb, in ascending order, the median would be number 50 on the list. It's commonly assumed that the median price is the same as the average price, but that's not the case. To calculate the average, you would add up the 100 sales and divide the total by 100 (the number of sales).
Mortgagor	The party borrowing funds whose property assets are mortgaged as security in favour of the lender.
Mortgagee	The lender of funds who takes mortgage security over the assets of the borrower.
Negatively geared	This is where the incomings are less than your outgoings after all tax deductions have been

claimed. For example, you receive rent of a property of $600 a month. Your shortfall is $300 a month, which you can claim as a loss when doing your tax return. Many people on high incomes use negative gearing to reduce their taxable income.

Off the plan When you buy off the plan, you are buying a property before it is built, having only seen the plans. This is commonly used for apartments or units under construction or about to be built.

Portfolio (as in property portfolio) The number and type of investment properties you own.

Positively geared This occurs when the investment income exceeds your interest expense (and other possible deductions). For example, the rent you receive may be $1000 a month, but the monthly repayments are only $750. Note that you may be subject to additional tax on any income derived from a positively geared investment.

Property cycle Property values usually follow a cycle of growth, a slowdown, a bust and an upturn. History shows that this occurs every seven to ten years.

Rental yields The return on an investment as a percentage of the amount invested. Gross rental yield can be calculated by multiplying the weekly rent by 52 (weeks in a year), then dividing by the value of the property and multiplying this figure by 100 to get the percentage.

Serviceability Whether you can manage your mortgage payments, based on your income and expenses.

Supply and demand The number of properties on the market at any given time determines the supply and demand equation. If there are lots of properties on the market, it's a buyers' market. If there are few properties on the market or those that come on to the market sell quickly, then it's a sellers' market.

Unconditional The point at which all conditional clauses within a sale and purchase or lease agreement have been satisfied or dispensed and the transaction is contractually binding on both parties.

Vacancy rates A measure of how many dwellings are available for rent over a specified time period. A low vacancy rate means there are not very many dwellings available for rent, while a high vacancy rate means there is ample supply of rental properties.

Valuation An estimation of the value of the security you are providing to the bank done by an independent professional valuer. The valuer is commissioned by the bank to conduct the valuation. The valuer takes into account the nature of the property being valued and recent sales of similar properties in the same area. Some lenders may not require valuations in certain circumstances.

Yield   income received from an asset

Testimonials

Since having the pleasure of meeting and being mentored by Helen and Ed, my husband and I have achieved a property portfolio of 7 properties worth a total of $2.50 million in three years.

Their unrelenting patience and dedication has brought our level of understanding in the area of property investment from novice to competence. I am confident that with further coaching from Helen and Ed, our property investment days have just begun!
Tania Morrison, Victoria

Previously it took me 6 years to purchase 2 investment properties. One year of mentoring from Real Wealth Australia resulted in my purchasing another 5 properties. They helped me to focus, gather momentum and fast-track my property portfolio. They also saved me from going through with a couple of purchases which would have been major costly mistakes. This is just as important as making successful profitable purchases.
Eliza Leung, New South Wales.

Helen and Ed share everything they have learned freely so we can skip some of the hurdles we would come up against if we were to take the property investing plunge on our own. They treat their clients more like friends so it's a very supportive, nurturing environment for the novices and a great forum for those more experienced to bounce off ideas and refine skills.
Tabitha Dougall, Victoria

We purchased our first property successfully only a couple of months into the program and it has already made us $30.000. We had looked at investing in property for a number of years but never felt that we had all the information we needed to make an informed decision. Now investing in property is so much simpler to understand. We are looking at purchasing our second investment property.
Amanda Mauro, Queensland

With Ed and Helen's guidance I have gone from owning 2 properties to purchasing a further 4 properties. Their mentoring has compelled me to take action and, more importantly, to have faith in my actions. I have learned from them the difference between being an educated investor and being someone who just purchases property. I am more confident, more certain and a better property investor because of them.
John Webb, Victoria

Ed and Helen have been fantastic in taking us through the investing process. Their practical approach to education and their unwavering focus on due diligence and risk management has given us the confidence and tools to start building our own property portfolio.

If you want to know how the property game is played, meet like-minded investors, and be challenged and stimulated while having the benefit and experience of two property gurus on your side, then their course is for you!
Richard & Sarah Hutchings, New South Wales

We have a lot of respect for Helen and Ed. They have acted on their dream of building abundance through property investing.

They've done the hard yards themselves, paid for their mistakes and are now celebrating their victories. A major focus for them has become sharing their knowledge to make a positive difference for us investors as we negotiate our way through the property investing maze. Helen and Ed have helped us with tightening up our due diligence, given us practical tips when negotiating and signing contracts on real life deals and connected us with other like-minded investors. We have felt comforted and reassured, knowing they are mentoring us through the process because they have been there and done it themselves. We are grateful that they have been so open with their knowledge and are inspired by the heart they have for people.

Grant & Lisa Owen, Victoria

The one-on-one mentoring sessions are really worth their weight in gold. Being able to put theory into practice for you personally by figuring out what works best for your situation is where the rubber really starts to hit the road.

Lisa Webb, Queensland

Ed and Helen's approach to financial freedom through real estate is different to all the others I have seen, both in Australia and New Zealand. It is not pie in the sky theories. You benefit from a collection of set backs, hard lessons and victories they have learned themselves as property investors. They had the determination and perhaps even desperation in their early years, to see their own goals through, to keep trying one more time, in an industry where most new players give up.

They will help you set and achieve goals you never thought possible, and along the way give you the encouragement you will

need and help you at each "obstacle" they know you will encounter, where others leave you floundering.
Phil Lohrey, Victoria

Helen and Ed have been a real inspiration for wealth creation, especially when you hear what they have done in such a short timeframe. Their sessions have certainly given me more knowledge about buying real estate, and mixing with like-minded people gives you the confidence and support to put your knowledge into practice in a positive way. No time like the present to start investing for the future!

Cheers to playing golf/tennis mid week with mates your own age at 40...
Angela Smith, New South Wales

About the author

Helen Collier-Kogtevs worked for many years in the corporate world and realised that her superannuation would not be enough to sustain a comfortable retirement. Starting with nothing, Helen, with her husband Ed, was able to build a multi-million dollar property portfolio. She spent many years learning and applying the knowledge gained through property investment courses and engaging mentors. This has led to the creation of Real Wealth Australia, which runs programs that educate investors on the principles of investing and provides mentoring to help people implement their investment strategy.

Helen is an author, educator and investor. Her passion for wanting to make a positive difference to people's lives inspired her to create mentoring programs that teach people how to build their own property investment portfolios. Helen writes for international and Australian newspapers and magazines. She is a presenter and speaker who enjoys sharing her knowledge and helping others travel their journey to financial abundance.